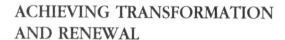

ACHIEVING TRANSFORMATION AND RENEWAL

IN FINANCIAL SERVICES

Achieving transformation and

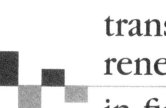

renewal

in financial services

Edited by Rohit Talwar

CRC Press
Boca Raton Boston New York Washington, DC

WOODHEAD PUBLISHING LIMITED
Cambridge England

Published by Woodhead Publishing Ltd
Abington Hall, Abington
Cambridge CB1 6AH
England

Published in North and South America by CRC Press LLC
2000 Corporate Blvd, NW
Boca Raton FL 33431
USA

First published 1999, Woodhead Publishing Ltd and CRC Press LLC

British Library Cataloguing in Publication Data
A catalogue record for this book is available from the British Library.

Library of Congress Cataloging in Publication Data
A catalog record for this book is available from the Library of Congress.

Woodhead Publishing ISBN 1 85573 433 8
CRC Press ISBN 0-8493-1755-X

CRC Press order number: WP1755

Cover design by The ColourStudio
Typeset by Best-set Typesetter Ltd, Hong Kong

Contents

Foreword ix

Series preface xii

Dedication xxiv

Contributors xxv

Introduction 1

1 Key management tools and techniques 14
Rohit Talwar

The Balanced Business Scorecard *14*
Business Process Re-engineering *15*
Participative approaches to change *25*
The attraction of participative approaches *26*
The mechanics of participation *26*
The underlying principles *28* References *28*

2 Managing change at Abbey National 30
Tim Murley

Introduction *30* Case studies *38* Conclusion *50*
Bibliography *51*

3 Building stronger customer relationships through the customer service chain 52
Ken Littlewood

The importance of customer loyalty *52*
The customer service chain *53*
Conclusion – integrating the service chain *58*
References *59*

4 Using the business excellence model to drive change 60
Leslie Ross

Introduction *60* The Mortgage Express turnaround *61*
A commitment to excellence *61*
Background to Mortgage Express *63*
The road to quality *63* The Balanced Scorecard *65*
Conclusion *83*

5 Using business process re-engineering to improve mortgage repayments 85
Chris Lazenby

Introduction *85* The company *86*
Economic background *86*
Business process re-engineering at Britannia *87*
Arrears collection *87* Strategy *88* Getting started *88*
Individuals and roles *89* Technology *90*
Management information and targets *91*
Structure *92* Achievements *92*
Extending re-engineering to other areas *93*

6 Managing innovation Part 1: Policies and products 95
Brian Fries

Introduction *95* Framework *97*
Model for managing change *102*
Product innovation *104* Quality *106* Summary *112*

7 Managing innovation Part 2: Processes 113
Brian Fries

Processes *113* Projects *126* Summary *133*

8 Business transformation at MLC 135
Oona Nielssen

What is MLC? *136* The market *136*
MLC's transformation *137*
Transformation triggers: marketplace, shareholders,

people *137* How MLC does business *138*
The transformation process *138*
Product simplification *139* Process simplification *140*
Cultural change *143* What happened – the cultural impact *145*
Staff reductions *145* The results of transformation *146*
Conclusion *146* References *147*

9 Using modern technology to build new capabilities **148**
Clive Holtham

Introduction *148* Frameworks *149*
Technology architecture *152* Managing legacy systems *153*
Identifying the technology's potential *154*
Moving from product-based to customer-based
  systems *155*
Reversing traditional management fears and concerns
  over IT *158*
Building new IT capabilities *158*
Changing the rules of the game through IT *160*
Leveraging the newly developed capabilities *162*
Conclusion *164* References *164*

10 Managing outsourcing and subcontracting **166**
Edmond Cunningham

The outsourcing debate – determining what is core and
  what is not *166*
Making the outsourcing decision – hard and
  soft factors *171*
When should you redesign the processes affected by
  outsourcing . . .? *175*
Preparing people, processes and systems for
  outsourcing *178*
Making the transition *180* Managing the contract *182*
Handling disputes *185* Managing consultants *185*
Conclusion *186* Notes *186* References *187*

11 Conclusion – New era, new challenges, new strategies **188**
Robit Talwar

People, processes and performance *188*
Real people, real change, real results *189*
The process decade *189*

Performance measurement *190*

21st century themes and challenges *190*

The emergence of the new economy *191*

Financial services via the Internet – hype, fact and fiction *200*

New entrants, new rules, new strategies *201*

Understanding the net generation *202*

Managing at the 'speed of change' *203*

Creating an infrastructure for accelerated change *203*

Conclusions – A 21st century survival guide *210*

References *210*

Appendix: Resources for transformation and renewal 211

Index 219

Foreword

by Sir Brian Pitman, Chairman,
Lloyds TSB Group plc

As we approach the millennium, it is beginning to dawn that we are in a new era – not merely a cyclical change, but a fundamental structural change. We're not managing evolution. What we are managing is transformation.

Preparing for the future has become a serious business throughout the corporate world. The essence of coping with change is anticipation. We all know that the future is unknowable. Yet, that should not be accepted as a cop out. The prizes will go to those who can see industry trends and then leverage it to their advantage. If you do not dictate the competition, someone else will. And then you will be on the back foot.

Technology will force the pace. Knowledge age organisations will require a different type of leadership from the industrial age organisation, to which we are accustomed. Old habits and beliefs must change. We shall need new ways of focusing resources to get maximum value in an age when knowledge moves at the speed of light.

No strategic analysis is likely to reveal any secret path to a risk-free future. The global environment for financial institutions will continue to be intermittently hazardous. There is, however, the opportunity for companies to alter their business structure in order to manage those hazards with greater confidence and to prepare themselves to withstand any sudden, unexpected blows.

We run a risk if we do something, but we also run a risk if we do nothing. The ultimate risk would be to do nothing at a time when the whole financial services industry is in transition.

What all this means for our people is enormous change. It has made our organisations less comfortable – and certainly less predictable – places to work in. People like the status quo. They like the way it was. When you start changing things, the good old days look better and better. You have to be prepared for massive resistance.

One of the main tasks of top management, by words and actions, will be to reinforce the company's objectives, strategy and value system. It is essential for the whole team to know and be committed to where we want to go and how we are going to get there. It is an unending task. But without such leadership, there is little chance of sustained, superior performance in a rapidly changing environment.

We cannot change behaviour simply by issuing instructions. We can only change behaviour, and therefore strategy, by changing beliefs.

Change requires:

● good, solid logic to justify the change

● real commitment, forged through sharing in the development of the logic and the creation of new beliefs, strategies and actions

● continued support, with new performance goals, incentives consistent with these goals, information flows which fit the new strategy and an organisational structure that helps to make the strategy happen.

The more the leader involves his team, the easier and better the change process, and the more likely that change will be continuous and productive. Success depends on people who understand and support the logic and then find ways to make it work, rather than back off or compromise as problems inevitably arise.

In times of turbulence and rapid change, it is hard to overemphasize the importance of candour – facing reality, seeing the world as it is rather than as you wish it were. People can take tough news. What they cannot take is deception.

The qualities required to succeed are open-mindedness, energy, the will to progress, commitment and flexibility. It means the unremitting pursuit of high standards of performance with a dedicated, long term, professional approach and a willingness to accept an endless process of change. The aim is to win, not just to improve.

I am often asked when I think our industry's transformation will be complete. The answer is simple: never.

Series preface

The theme of this book series is *Managing Change in Financial Services*. In this introduction I would like to explain why this series will provide fascinating reading, valuable insights and useful case material, not just for executives and policy-makers in banking, insurance, and capital markets, but also for managers in other industries which are taking the same path towards globalisation, electronic commerce, and faster-moving markets. Financial services businesses are leading the way towards the global economy because capital can be moved around more easily and more quickly than either labour, raw materials or goods and services. In fact, as Peter Drucker has pointed out 'financial markets have become de-coupled from the world economy'. But where financial services is today, other industries – like electronics, computers, telecommunications, and air transport – will be in the near future. Looking to the future Jack Welch, the Chairman and Chief Executive Officer of General Electric envisages more intensive competition on a global scale: 'Ahead of us are Darwinian shake-outs in every major marketplace with no consolation prizes for the losing companies and nations'.

[1] *Business Week*, 24–31 August, 1998.

In this introduction to the series I would like to review the following issues:

● What are the driving forces behind the revolution which is occurring in financial services?

● How are the industry structures changing?

● Why are we seeing such chaos in financial markets?

● What kinds of solutions might be found?

● What are the challenges for managers in adapting their organisations to these turbulent markets?

● How does the book series aim to help managers in coping with these problems?

The driving forces

In recent years the financial services industry has been hit by three major trends:

● deregulation and privatisation,

● the introduction of new technologies and new products, and

● the entry of new competitors from other countries, and other industries.

Deregulation and privatisation

In the name of open competition, trading in currencies, stocks and shares, and commodities has been deregulated, and many national markets in banking and insurance have been opened up to international competition – globally or across regional trading blocs such as the European Community, ASEAN or NAFTA. We have also seen the opening up of former communist and emerging economies in Russia, Eastern Europe, China and South East Asia.

Over the same period state-owned banks and Post Office Giros have been privatised and savings banks and mutual building societies have become public listed companies.

New technologies and new products

Also, the speed of change has been accelerated through the introduction of electronic markets for stocks and shares, currencies and commodities, and the establishment of 24-hour markets for financial services by telephone, and on the Internet.

Meanwhile, investment bankers have developed new products, generally known as 'derivatives', which enable individuals and organisations to gamble on the likely future value of currencies, stocks and shares or commodities which multiplies the profits and the risks of each deal.

New competitors

The effect of opening up markets in former communist countries, in developing economies, and in regional free-trade areas like the European Community has been to promote cross-border competition and to create global markets. London, for example, plays host to 500 foreign banks, and the leading British bank, The Hong Kong & Shanghai Bank, is now partly owned by the Chinese government.

Also, in Britain and elsewhere, major 'non-banks' have entered retail banking and insurance markets in the form of:

● *retail multiples* like Marks & Spencer and Tesco,

● *direct operators* like Direct Line and Virgin, who have no branches but sell financial services by press advertising, direct mail and telephone,

● *Internet companies* who offer banking, insurance and stockbroking services by computer.

Changes in industry structures

The opening up of financial markets during the 1990s had profound effects on the financial services industry and also on national economies. We have seen unprecedented growth in the demand for financial services, intense competition on a world scale and the emergence of very large global companies.

Financial conglomerates

1998 saw mega-mergers between some major US banking groups:

- Travelers Group and Citicorp valued at $75.5 billion,

- Norwest and Wells Fargo valued at $34 billion, and

- Banc One and First Chicago valued at $25 billion.

Also, in 1998 the Swiss Bank Corporation acquired the Union Bank of Switzerland for $80 billion.

These followed large mergers in Britain – between Hong Kong & Shanghai Banking Corporation (HSBC) and Midland, and between Lloyds Bank and TSB. Now all eyes are on NatWest Group, Barclays Bank, Halifax and the former building societies.

Table 1 shows the size and profitability of the largest European banks after the latest round of mergers.

Investment banking

Investment banking has also seen a spate of mergers. Since the beginning of 1997 a whole tier of US investment banks has taken advantage of record prices to sell out to larger US and European banks. In the UK NatWest Markets, BZW, Hambros and Guinness Mahon have been dismembered or sold. The larger US investment banks are now beginning to merge, as we see with the uniting of

Table 1 Europe's biggest banks

	Total assets, billion dollars	Estimated return on equity in 1998, %
UBS	754	19.9
Deutsche Bank	596	7.2*
Credit Suisse	479	15.5
HSBC	472	16.7
Hypovereinsbank	464	9.6
Credit Agricole	429	NA
Societe Generale	420	13.0
ABN AMRO	414	17.1
Barclays	392	18.3

*Excludes Daimler Benz special dividend
DATA J.P. Morgan & Co, Solomon Smith Barney, *Business Week*, September 21, 1998

Solomon Brothers and Smith Barney, and the linking of Morgan Stanley with Dean Witter.

Insurance

In 1997 Royal Insurance and Sun Alliance came together and speculation began to grow about Prudential and Norwich Union.

1997/1998 was also a momentous time in insurance broking. Marsh & McLennan, the world's largest insurance broker took over Sedgwick – the third largest. Willis Corroon, the fourth largest, was acquired by Kohlberg Kravis Roberts, and Aon, another US company, took over Alexander & Alexander. These deals were the latest in a 3-year round of consolidation that has folded a dozen or so big insurance brokers into three. It is now estimated that Marsh & McLennan, Aon, Willis Corroon, and Arthur J Gallagher place 80% of total brokered business.[2]

The reinsurance industry is already highly concentrated with the four top companies, Munich Re, Swiss Re, General Re, and Employers Re, sharing half of the market, and five others – including Lloyds of London – sharing the next 26%.[3]

The chaos in financial markets

The development of freer, more global financial markets with 24-hour on-screen trading has accelerated the pace of change and increased volatility in the prices of securities, commodities and national currencies. In the past decade, one government after another has found its currency attacked by speculators and devalued – Britain, Italy, Spain, Mexico, Japan, the emerging countries of South East Asia and Russia.

The year to August 1998 saw a catastrophic collapse in the currencies of South East Asia – measured against the US dollar:

Indonesian Rupiah	− 80.6%
South Korean Won	− 33.3%
Thai Baht	− 26.3%
Taiwan Dollar	− 16.0%[4]

[2] Paula Hawkins, Policy Brokers Rush to Consolidate Risk, *The European*, 31 August, 6 September, 1998.
[3] Standard & Poor's Re-insurance: The Hidden Insurance Market (1997), *Business Week*, 14 September, 1998.
[4] Bloomberg Financial Markets, quoted in *Business Week*, 31 August, 1998, p. 16.

Also, over the year to July 1998, share prices in 'emerging stock markets' measured in US dollars by the IFC index declined by around 50%, and shares in South East Asia and Russia dropped by over 80%.[5]

The falling values in currencies and stock markets were accompanied in these regions by dramatic falls in the prices of manufactured products, commodities, and real estate.

In Hong Kong, by early September 1998, the economy was contracting at 4% per annum, share prices had lost $300 billion in the past year and property values had declined by around $250 billion, and were expected to fall another 50%. This left Hong Kong banks, which had 44% of their loans in real estate, perilously exposed. High interest rates for short term loans, which rose to 12.33% at the end of August, from 7.36% a year earlier, were squeezing both the banks and their borrowers.[6] The turbulence in Asia and Russia has even affected Latin American markets: the Brazilian market lost 40% in August; Mexico and Argentina were down by a half since January, and Chile was at its lowest level since 1993. Latin America's weakest link was Venezuela where stocks were down 72% in dollar terms. Low oil prices had reduced government revenues sending short-term interest rates above 100% and the weakening bolivar was a candidate for devaluation before year-end.[7]

Bank losses

The banking industry is at the epicentre of this market collapse – the Western banks because they encouraged companies, and individuals, in North America and Europe to invest their money in Russia, South East Asia, and other emerging markets – and the banks of Russia and South East Asia because they accepted the money and financed local projects, although they were in many cases grossly over-committed and they did not honestly report the high level of their debts, and losses.

Russia's decision to default on the equivalent of US$49 billion of debt will hit Western banks particularly hard. Bank America, Chase Manhattan and Citicorp stand to lose around $6.8 billion; the German banks are collectively owed $30.5 billion; and the combined losses

---

[5] *The Economist*, 22 August 1998, p.62.
[6] Mark L Clifford, Is Hong Kong a Free Market?, *Business Week*, 14 September, 1998.
[7] Ian Katz and Elizabeth Malkin, Latin America: More Where That Came From, *Business Week*, 14 September 1998.

of UBS and Credit Suisse are estimated to be over $400 million. In Britain, Barclays Capital is expected to lose $544 million.[8]

The leading investment banks, who were successful salesmen for 'emerging market securities', are now announcing their losses. Merrill Lynch declared $135 million 'emerging market losses' in the third quarter of 1998. Credit Suisse First Boston admitted a $254 million cut in profits, and ING Barings announced 250 layoffs, and signalled the need for a further 25% cut in costs.[9]

Fraud, corruption and lack of control

The Western media are full of articles analysing the underlying causes for the decline of the Russian, the South East Asian and the Japanese economies. The reasons are many and various, ranging from blatant fraud and corruption in Russia, and some South East Asian countries, to the need for tighter controls and better corporate governance in Japan.

A major problem in Japan is inaccurate reporting of company results. The Japanese banks are thought to be holding at least $600 billion worth of suspect loans guaranteed almost exclusively by land. Land prices have fallen for the past six years and residential land is now worth less than half of what it was worth in 1992. But most of the banks are still carrying this land on their books at 70% of its peak value – not 50%, which is its real value. They need to increase their provisions for these loans by at least a third but they cannot afford to do this.[10]

The search for solutions

Government officials and business leaders in the 'emerging countries' are staggered by the sharp impact of the short-term flow of hot money around world financial markets. They complain about the activities of Western speculators which have devalued their currencies, securities and commodities, and they are searching for ways to

[8] *The European*, 31 August–6 September, 1998, p.48 (Source: Bank for International Settlements), and Paula Hawkins, Fortress Europe Fight Contagion, *The European*, 7–13 September, 1998.

[9] Anita Raghavan, Emerging Markets Wreak Havoc on Merrill's Profits, *Wall Street Journal Europe*, 9 September, 1998.

[10] Brian Bremner and Mark L Clifford, The Walls Go Up, *Business Week*, 14 September, 1998.

defend their capital markets, and their companies, from the representatives of Western banks who are now trying to buy their assets
at bargain basement prices.

The solutions being sought are different in each country, but there
is a general recognition of the need to impose local controls, and to
try to re-regulate their financial markets rather than simply forcing
their banks and companies into bankruptcy. Malaysia has imposed
exchange controls and both Hong Kong and Taiwan have intervened
in their financial markets to curb the activities of speculators.

There is a general reluctance to follow the instructions of Western
advisers and let their weaker banks go bankrupt:

In Thailand where the banks have reported record losses, led
by Bangkok Bank's $400 million, the Thai government is reported
to be considering nationalising all but a handful of the country's
15 banks.[11]

In Japan the government is afraid that bank failures might set
off a chain reaction of corporate bankruptcies – as happened
when Hokkaido Takushoku Bank failed in 1997. Instead, regulators are encouraging strong banks like Sumitomo Trust & Banking
Co to merge with weaker banks such as The Credit Bank of Japan
Ltd.[12]

Policy makers know that newly industrialising economies need
access to international capital markets, and to the latest technology,
but they must find ways of restricting the size of loans which local
banks can raise in foreign currencies. International regulations
also need attention. What Alan Greenspan calls 'the patchwork of
arrangements and conventions to govern the international financial
system' has not kept pace with the technological developments.[13]

In Russia particularly, but also in many other emerging markets,
stronger corporate governance systems are required to ensure that
the top managers of banks and industrial companies do not treat
company assets as their own personal capital but act as responsible
stewards working on behalf of shareholders, creditors, employees
and other parties with a legitimate interest in their businesses. In
many countries this will require changes in board structures, company relations with shareholders, employees and customers, and a

---

[11] Bruce Einhorn & Ron Carben, Thailand Banking Chaos, *Business Week*, 17 August, 1998.
[12] Brian Bremner and Mark L Clifford, The Walls Go Up', *Business Week*, 14 September, 1998.
[13] For a description of the 'new world order' which is required for financial services see: Jeffrey
Sachs, Global Capitalism: Making it Work', *The Economist*, 12 September, 1998.

new generation of responsible managers supported by the power of law.

In Japan, too, corporate governance needs to be reformed in three key areas:

Cross-shareholdings

About 50% of shares of companies on the Tokyo Stock Market are held by other industrial or financial groups. This makes them virtually invulnerable to takeover.

Lack of financial transparency

The financial reports of Japanese companies are not explicit. The financial businesses which recently went bankrupt – Hokkaido Takushoku Bank and Yamaichi Securities – had much larger liabilities than they had reported. Many groups have bad debts in subsidiaries which are not shown on their balance sheets.

Management accountability

The existing management in a badly performing Japanese company often expect to keep their jobs although they are not producing good results. Often, too, Japanese managers are not used to producing returns for shareholders.[14]

The challenge for business leaders

The impact of the global changes taking place in financial services will be to reduce profits, to increase market volatility and risk, and to encourage organisations to arrange ever larger mergers and acquisitions in an effort to cut costs and share risks. Heavier competition and narrower margins will also force management to abandon non-performing businesses and focus on those activities where they can produce a world-class performance.

The major challenge for European banks is to position themselves for EMU. Some analysts estimate that the European banking business may shrink by 200,000 to 500,000 jobs within a few years and in a decade perhaps only a dozen mammoth financial institutions may remain.[15]

Recent studies by McKinsey and by US investment banks[16] suggest

[14] Paul Abrahams, Foreigners Flood In, *Financial Times*, 26 June, 1998.
[15] Stanley Reed, Bank Eat Bank, *Business Week*, 21 September, 1998.
[16] See Thane Peterson, Bank Eat Bank, *Business Week*, 21 September, 1998.

that in the next three to five years European banks' profits will come under severe pressure:

Corporate lending
European revenues from corporate lending will be cut nearly in half to $50 billion as ever smaller companies demand discounts.

Foreign exchange
In the years following the arrival of the euro in January 1999, 70% of European banks' foreign exchange revenues, which represent about 5% of a typical bank's earnings, will disappear.

The bond market
Meanwhile, fiscal controls imposed by the monetary union means that governments will issue fewer bonds.

Asset management
If, as a result of the present crisis, there is a prolonged bear market in stocks and shares, there will be lower growth in unit trusts and asset management services, and Europe's high money-management fees – about double the US level – will be reduced by heightened competition.

Specialisation
As a result, most European banks will have to focus on a few major businesses, and compete aggressively in these areas: Banks will have to specialise in businesses where they can compete across Europe. Only a few 'investment' banks, like Lazard Frères or Paribas will be able to compete with Goldman Sachs or Morgan Stanley.

Withdrawals from investment banking
In the 1990s, many European banks followed a strategy of 'globalisation through heavy investment in capital markets' such as investment banking, asset management and other securities-based businesses. Deutsche Bank is estimated to have invested $3 billion in investment banking but the results have been disappointing. British banks like Barclays and NatWest have already dropped out. Continental banks like Deutsche and Dresdner know that to survive they will have to double their investments to compete with US banks like Goldman Sachs, Merrill Lynch and Salomon which have established powerful organisations in Europe.[17]

---

[17] Stanley Reed, Where's the Bonanza?, *Business Week*, 21 September, 1998.

Mergers and restructuring

The major cost reductions are expected to come from more big mergers between domestic banks. JP Morgan estimates that $102 billion in value could be released by bank mergers – through staff cuts, branch closures, merging computer systems and eliminating overlaps.

Banks vulnerable to takeover

The losses resulting from plunging stock markets and financial crises overseas could make many banks vulnerable to takeover. Union Bank of Switzerland came under pressure to merge with Swiss Bank Corporation because in 1997 the bank lost $443 million in derivative trading losses in Asia. Barclays Bank lost $418 million in emerging markets in the first half of 1998. Analysts estimate that Credit Suisse lost up to $700 million in Russian government bonds in August 1998. As a result of losses like these the value of most bank shares in Europe has declined by a third from their 1998 peaks, but other bank shares like UBS and ABN Amro are up in expectation of further mergers.

Managing change in financial services

In this context we are launching this series of books on *Managing change in financial services*. The first three books will cover:

- *Driving strategic change in financial services*

- *Developing people and culture in financial services*

- *Achieving transformation and renewal in financial services*

Each aims to provide, through close analysis of the issues and case studies written by leading figures in the financial services sector worldwide, blueprints for the management of change across this fast-changing and fast-converging industry. Throughout, the emphasis is on the practical implementation of change management strategies, as employed by those who are at the cutting edge of change in the international financial services community today.

Future titles in the series will continue to focus on key strategic issues for the financial services sector in the new millennium, and potential authors are invited to contact the publishers direct at Woodhead Publishing Ltd, Abington Hall, Abington, Cambridge CB1 6AH, England, tel: +44 (0)1223 891358; fax: +44 (0)1223 893694; e-mail: wp@woodhead-publishing.com.

Bernard Taylor
Emeritus Professor of Strategic Management
Henley Management College

A DEDICATION TO DENIS BOYLE

The volume *Developing people and culture in financial services* in this series was edited by Denis Boyle, the Managing Director of Service Management Systems (UK). SMS, which was founded in the 1970s by the Swedish consultant Richard Normann, was the *first* consultancy to specialise in the management of service businesses. Denis Boyle established SMS in Britain and worked closely with many European service businesses. His clients included Fiat, major Italian, Swedish and British banks, the Prudential and other insurance companies.

For over 20 years, as a consultant to top management, Denis was deeply involved with managing change in large organisations, and in the 1990s he was closely associated in this work with The Tom Peters Organisation.

Tragically, Denis Boyle died during the development of this series. He was concerned from the beginning in the creation of the series and we, his co-editors, would like to dedicate the series to the memory of Denis Boyle as a good friend and colleague, and as a tribute to his pioneering work in helping to create and develop the new field of Service Management.

Bernard Taylor, Ian Morison, Rohit Talwar and Vlad Stanić

Contributors

Edmond Cunningham

Edmond Cunningham is the current elected Chairman of the Computing Services and Software Association (CSSA) Outsourcing Group. He is a Principal Consultant with PA Consulting Group. At the time of writing, he was a consultant with Unisys Ltd in the outsourcing practice. Edmond's career in IT encompasses roles in programme management, systems integration, project management, outsourcing and service management consulting. Edmond has worked in outsourcing since 1992. He holds a Bachelor of Commerce degree and an MBA from Cranfield (1992). He is a member of AMBA, the Strategic Planning Society and a Fellow of the RSA.

Brian Fries

Brian Fries is currently Vice President responsible for Project and Quality Management at Chase Manhattan. He was in charge of the European Integration Office, overseeing the merger of Chemical Bank with Chase. This involved establishing consistent project management methodologies, monitoring progress of critical projects and risks, reporting to senior management locally and in New York, and facilitating and assisting the many project teams, as appropriate.

He originally qualified as a Chartered Accountant in London, after which he worked for Price Waterhouse in Germany. In his final position, he managed their Computer and Systems Audit Department, which had staff in five separate offices throughout the country, and played a significant role in co-ordinating systems activities for major clients throughout Europe. As a result, he gained extensive experience of working with many multinational corporations, including Chevron Oil, Du Pont, Hewlett Packard and IBM, who were using distributed processing technology to develop consistent management and reporting systems in the different countries and cultures of Europe at that time.

He returned to the UK in 1983 and joined the International Auditing Department of Manufacturers Hanover to manage their Computer Audit group, with responsibility for UK, Europe, Middle East and South America. During the merger with Chemical Bank in 1992/93, Auditing acted as consultants to management on many diverse control issues affecting the restructuring of businesses and operating departments, system changes and the development of new organisational policies and procedures.

In 1994, Brian was a founder member of Chemical Bank's Project and Quality Management Group, established to raise standards, facilitate the management of cross-functional projects throughout the UK, introduce a quality programme into the bank and generally act as internal consultants and agents of change in the new organization.

Clive Holtham

After taking a Master's degree in management, Clive Holtham trained as an accountant and was Young Accountant of the Year in 1976. Following six years as a Director of Finance and IT he moved to the City University Business School in 1988.

He carried out a major research project for the Institute of Directors, examining the IT needs of executives and he authored *Executive Information Systems and Decision Support* (Chapman and Hall, 1992). His 1993 research study, *Improving the Performance of Workgroups through Information Technology*, has become a bestseller and has been translated into French. He has also written a large number of other publications.

He lectures, broadcasts and consults in the UK, USA and continental Europe and is the research director of the BFS (Business Facilitation System) research project, developing an intensively computer-supported meeting environment for managers and executives. He is co-director of the Paperless Knowledge Worker project, which involves detailed examination of the effect of digitizing the paper files of a management consultant. A co-founder of the University's Multimedia Research Group, he has been reviewing the strategic impact of both CD-ROM and networked multimedia on business internationally.

Chris Lazenby

After graduating in engineering from Queen Mary College, University of London, Chris Lazenby worked as an actuarial student, a financial analyst and a project manager before he settled on a career in information technology. A Chartered Engineer and member of the British Computing Society, he has spent over twenty years in systems with major companies such as Massey-Ferguson, Ladbrokes and Lunn Poly. He joined Britannia Building Society as their Group Head of Information Systems in 1992, taking responsibility for enabling business change through technology. He now leads Britannia's Business Improvement department, which controls all significant projects throughout the business.

Ken Littlewood

Ken Littlewood has worked in the financial services industry for over 20 years, mostly with Midland Bank, where for the 6 years until the end of 1996 he was Head of Network Development and responsible for their branch network location and investment strategy and their customer service programmes. In 1997 he joined Sabanci Bank, a privately owned Turkish bank based in London, as head of their operations.

Prior to this he worked in the airline industry for British Airways, including several years based in New York. Over the last 10 years he has worked with a number of leading UK Business Schools and is currently a member of the MBA course team with the Open University Business School. He is a Chairman of the Strategic Planning Society in the UK and a Board Director of the Strategic Leadership Forum in North America.

Tim Murley

As Abbey National's Director of Strategic Performance Improvement, Tim Murley is responsible for the company's internal management consultancy, project management, procurement strategy and centralised procurement activities. Previously, he was Head of Banking Operations and Head of Management Accounting at Abbey National. Prior to joining Abbey National, Mr Murley was adviser and personal assistant to His Excellency the Minister of Housing, State of Bahrain.

Oona Nielssen

Oona Nielssen has worked for Lend Lease since 1997. She was recently appointed as Global Communications Manager for Lend Lease Property. She has consulted internationally on communications, strategy, learning and change. Before joining Lend Lease she worked for many years in broadcasting, adult education and in theatre. Oona has worked in Australia, South Africa, USA, the Pacific and Europe on leadership development, media training, organisational development and workplace change.

Leslie Ross

After graduating with a degree in geography, Leslie Ross spent ten years with the Nationwide Building Society. He progressed from Graduate Trainee through a period in Branch Management, to a role of project co-ordinator for the Society's Automated Teller Machine (ATM) Project.

He joined TSB Group in 1987 as Project Manager, and shortly after moved to Mortgage Express to lead the business analysis function in IT. In 1991 he was promoted to the Board and has been responsible for the Company's development programme and IT management.

Along with his Board colleagues at Mortgage Express he took a leading role in Mortgage Express's total quality management journey which included winning the UK Quality Award in 1996.

During 1997 Mortgage Express was sold to the Bradford and Bingley Building Society, where Leslie is now the Head of IT Architecture with responsibility for architecture and planning.

Leslie Ross would like to thank Keith Greenough for his help and guidance over the years and for contributing material for his chapter.

Rohit Talwar

Rohit Talwar is an experienced adviser, facilitator and trainer working in the fields of strategic management and organisational transformation. He is the founder of FastFuture – the Centre for Business Transformation, which works mainly with major organisations in the financial services, electronics, information technology and telecommunications industries. Acting as a 21st century tour guide, his work focuses on:

- Accelerated scenario planning, strategy development and business innovation
- Assessing the strategic potential of the Internet and e-commerce
- Designing and facilitating programmes of organisational transformation and renewal
- The use of highly participative large group processes to accelerate the implementation of change
- Coaching and supporting project sponsors, senior management and project teams undertaking strategic transformation initiatives

He is an adviser to start-up technology companies for the UK Prince's Youth Business Trust and served as a non-executive director for one of the UK's largest Health Authorities where he had special responsibility for quality and innovation.

Previously he headed Bossard UK's Organisation and Process Management Consulting Group and was a Senior Consultant with Andersen Consulting. He has also worked for GKN, BT and Omron Tateisi in Japan.

Introduction – preparing for an uncertain future

Rohit Talwar, Director FastFuture –
The Centre for Business
Transformation

The case for change

Scan the business press, attend a management conference or tune into an Internet discussion. Whatever the source of your information and inspiration the main message you hear will be very similar. In short, organisations and industries the world over are facing an increasingly complex, networked and fast changing environment. The rules for survival and success have never been so unclear, the choice of strategies so uncertain and the pressure to act quickly so immense.

Given the backdrop of turbulence, rapid technological development and constant change, there is a key question for players in the financial services industry. That question is *'how do we develop the necessary flexibility and capability to enable us to serve our customers, employees and shareholders into the next century?'*

This series on *Managing Change in Financial Services* is designed to bring together the latest thinking on how organisations are addressing those issues in three distinct areas – crafting of business strategies, development of people and culture and achieving organisational transformation and renewal. In this book we focus on cases and concepts that describe how leading financial services organisations are trying to address the third of those perspectives.

This book is designed to be a practical handbook for transformation and renewal and draws on detailed case examples from Abbey National, Midland Bank, Mortgage Express, Britannia Building Society, Chemical Bank (now part of Chase Manhattan), MLC Australia, TSB and Western Provident Association. The cases provide a rich source of reference material describing how they are rethinking and reshaping their business operations to deliver the improvements in speed, cost of operations, service, quality, flexibility and the capacity to innovate required to ensure that they remain competitive and create businesses fit for purpose in the 21st century.

The structure of this book

The primary purpose of this book is to provide readers with a range of examples, practical techniques and insights to help them address the challenges they face in their own organisations. As such the emphasis is on the presentation of the cases themselves rather than a detailed analysis or critique of the approaches. Hence the majority of the cases are written by people from the organisations discussed and the rest are based on input provided by the case study organisations.

Hence the book is structured in the following way:

- The remainder of this introduction describes some of the specific challenges facing the case study organisations in this book and provides a summary of each of its chapters
- Chapter 1 provides an introduction to some of the main management tools and techniques used in the case study organisations
- In Chapters 2 through 8 the case study organisations describe their approaches to transformation and renewal
- Chapter 9 looks at the role of information technology in the change process
- In Chapter 10 the growing role of outsourcing as a mechanism for change is examined
- Chapter 11 breaks with the traditional format for conclusions and instead looks forward to the twenty-first century and examines some of the strategic implications of competing in a continuously changing 'wired world'. It then goes on to examine how organisations and individuals alike can survive and thrive in such a turbulent environment

⬤ In the Appendix we present a list of websites, books, magazines and organisations that may provide useful resources to support an organisational change process.

Addressing the change management challenges

As we will see, not all of the companies started from the same point or tackled the same challenges – indeed the spectrum ranges from continuous improvement through to crisis led turnaround. In chapters from Tim Murley of Abbey National and Brian Fries of Chemical Bank we learn how they have been reshaping their businesses to ensure continued success. In the case of Britannia Building Society, Chris Lazenby explains how they have responded to the particular challenges of reducing the losses from arrears on mortgage subscriptions. From Ken Littlewood we will hear how Midland Bank has been using a service-oriented approach to increase customer retention.

In the Mortgage Express case, Leslie Ross examines how the organisation set about transforming itself from a major loss maker to become a highly profitable entity and winner of the UK quality award. In Oona Nielssen's chapter we will see a remarkable story of employee driven transformation at MLC, the financial services arm of Lend Lease, an Australian based global property and funds management company.

Finally we have two independent perspectives on how the sector is seeking to build new capabilities and increase efficiency. Professor Clive Holtham describes the role of information technology in the transformation process and from Edmond Cunningham we hear how outsourcing is playing an increasing role in the drive to achieve competitive advantage.

Key drivers for change

Running through the cases are a number of common themes about the combination of internal and external drivers that have forced these organisations to review and reshape their operations. The most prevalent amongst these are summarised below.

Key external challenges

Regulatory changes

● *Deregulation encouraging new competitors* such as Virgin and Marks and Spencer to enter the marketplace bringing with them expertise honed in different sectors and a different approach to sales and service;

● *Increased regulatory control* over product design, conduct of transactions and reporting.

Market pressures

● *Growing customer sophistication* – financial services companies are beginning to recognise that they are not being judged against the best of the competition but against the best of all of the other product and services providers used by their customers;

● *A recession induced collapse of demand in core markets;*

● *Globalisation of markets and customers* which have created a growing realisation that in order to survive firms must judge themselves against World Class standards rather than just the local competition; the Internet is helping make these standards visible to all;

● *A growing emphasis on the need for speed* – product lifecycles are shortening and there is a greater willingness amongst customers to switch their business to better service providers; Internet-based services have further increased the pressure for firms to react quickly to customer requirements and opportunities in the marketplace.

Competitive challenges

● *Growing competition* from traditional players extending their product offerings and crossing the boundaries into related fields; for example, most building societies now offer life insurance products and many insurers are entering the instant access savings market;

● *New forms of competition* created through joint ventures such as the formation of Sainsbury's Bank – which uses the retailer's brand name and value proposition supported by the operational capabilities of the Royal Bank of Scotland and underpinned by a well managed technology infrastructure.

● *Over capacity* in many areas of the sector, often resulting from over optimistic strategies; a second cause is failure to support these infrastructure developments with the necessary investments in product development, marketing and service design;

● *Technology driven changes* that have enabled the creation of direct sales and service operations – often by players who are not tied to heavy past investments in premises and technology; most of the major players in retail financial services have been forced to follow the lead set by Direct Line in insurance and First Direct in banking; finally, rapid growth in web-based services and major investments in online banking from Citibank and others suggest the Internet and Digital Television offer the opportunity to bring about a complete revolution in the distribution of financial services products.

Key internal challenges

Stuctural and organisational pressures

● *Demutualisation* of players in the insurance and building society sectors which have introduced new shareholders demanding market rates of return on their investments;

● *Acquisitions and mergers* which have resulted in duplication of many functions and processes and which create the challenge of bringing together organisations with differing strategies, cultures and ways of working;

● *Outdated, slow and complex processes* – the literature is full of cases of organisations that failed to streamline their processes and take advantage of the opportunities created by technology; for example in the Western Provident Association case discussed later in this chapter, the organisation found that it was taking 28 days to perform 45 minutes of actual work required to process a new client application.

Cultural drivers

- *Complacency* over customer service and quality resulting from the failure of many organisations to look at themselves 'through the eyes of the customer';

- *Failure to reap the return on investment in information technology* often resulting from a lack of attention to the people, process and structural implications of technology based change; many have also found that earlier technical choices and a short termist approach to the management of this strategic resource has left them with 'legacy systems' which cannot be extended or adapted to changing business requirements;

- *Deeply embedded cultural and structural problems* resulting from organisations failing to adapt quickly enough to a changing world and an increasingly competitive marketplace;

The combined effect of these forces helps us understand why many of the organisations appearing in this book have done far more than simply change their processes and internal structures. In most cases, the response has needed to be more holistic, encompassing the culture, people, skills, attitudes, processes, systems, performance measures and management structures. Whether by design or necessity, they have all embarked on a never-ending journey of transformation and renewal.

Cases studies and perspectives

The following is a brief summary of the main chapters in this book.

Chapter 1 – Key management tools and techniques – Rohit Talwar

This chapter provides a short introduction to the Balanced Business Scorecard and Business Process Re-engineering – two of the tools and techniques most frequently adopted by the case study organisations in this book. Many of the case studies also make explicit or implicit references to the use of participative approaches to change.

A short overview of the benefits, rationale, mechanics and underlying principles of participation is provided. The application of these approaches is highlighted through the use of mini-cases on Western Provident Association and TSB.

Chapter 2 – Managing change at Abbey National - Tim Murley – Director, Strategic Performance Improvement

When judged by almost any measure of performance, Abbey National is rated as a highly successful organisation. Having converted from a Building Society to a Bank in 1989, its share price rose from 130p to 765p by the end of 1996 with a total annual shareholder return of over 28% per annum – ranking it second in the FT-SE 100. Underpinning this success has been a process of continuous refinement and review of all aspects of its operations.

At the heart of Abbey's management decision making and performance improvement strategy is a commitment to the creation of value for shareholders. In pursuit of this goal, Abbey has adopted the approach of Value Based Management to drive this focus on value creation. However, Abbey also recognises that non-financial measures have a direct impact on financial performance and has adopted the use of the Balanced Business Scorecard (BBS). Use of the BBS ensures that management focuses attention on i) customers, ii) innovation and improvement and iii) internal processes, alongside their impact on iv) financial measurements.

Tim Murley explains Abbey's approach to strategic performance improvement and the management of change in support of BBS targets. He also presents specific case examples of the application of a range of techniques and approaches including benchmarking, activity based costing, best practice reviews, process improvement and service quality management.

Chapter 3 – Building stronger customer relationships through the customer service chain – Ken Littlewood – Formerly Head of Network Development – Midland Bank

With the intensification of competition in retail financial services, the danger for an organisation such as Midland Bank is that other providers will target the most profitable parts of the service proposition for personal customers. In particular, technology is enabling new entrants to reduce transaction costs and is dramatically reducing the opportunity for sustainable product differentiation.

Under these circumstances, the key source of competitive advantage for banks and building societies is the quality of the relationship with the existing customer base. Across the sector, customer service is acknowledged as a key driver of customer retention or defection and hence profitability. To address these challenges, Midland has adopted the concept of the Service Profit Chain.

The Service Chain model suggests that 'internal service quality' (the quality of support to staff) drives employee satisfaction which in turn is a key driver of 'external service quality' (customer service) and hence customer satisfaction. Adopting the service chain approach has helped Midland improve satisfaction and retention levels, increase market share and raise the profile of service throughout the organisation.

Ken Littlewood explains how the key elements of the service chain have been used within Midland to develop and co-ordinate service quality initiatives. He highlights the critical importance of establishing 'listening posts' at each stage in the chain and describes the experience gained in managing each element of the chain.

Chapter 4 – Using the business excellence model to drive change in Mortgage Express – Leslie Ross – formerly Director of Business Services – Mortgage Express

Mortage Express was established in 1986 as a subsidiary of TSB Bank plc. with the objective of creating a low cost centralised lending operation offering a fast and more convenient service than branch based competitors. Following early success the company went into decline and in 1991–92 posted a loss of £100M. TSB made the decision that Mortgage Express should stop taking new business and withdraw from the market over the next two to three years.

Since then the company has undergone a remarkable turnaround. In the period from 1993–1996 customer satisfaction has improved from 70% to 95%, retention rates have increased, employee satisfaction is well above the national average and the company made profits of £104M over the period from 1993–96. The remarkable nature of the turnaround was acknowledged when Mortgage Express became joint winners of the British Quality Award for 1996.

Leslie Ross describes how this transformation was achieved and how the Business Excellence Model was used as a basis for continuous review and improvement of all aspects of the business. He explains how the goals of business excellence have been achieved through a combination of investment and belief in people, commitment to quality, challenging every aspect of the operations and a major communications programme.

Chapter 5 – Using business process re-engineering to improve mortgage repayments – Chris Lazenby – Head of Business Improvement – Britannia Building Society

The collection of mortgage payment arrears is a sensitive and unpleasant task. The recession in the early 1990s led to large increases in the number of customers falling into difficulties over repayments and caused major difficulties for many of the mortgage lenders.

In late 1992, with provisions for arrears and bad debts rising to unprecedented levels, Britannia decided to address the situation through a systematic review of the debt collection process. Over a period of two years, Britannia's re-engineering exercise totally revamped the debt collection operation to improve both effectiveness and customer sensitivity. As a result, debt provisions have been reduced from 20% above the industry norm to 20% below it.

Chris Lazenby describes how Britannia re-engineered its debt collection processes and shifted its philosophy from one of letter writing to direct customer contact. He explains how every aspect of the operation needed to be rethought and revamped as part of the change process.

Chapter 6 – Managing innovation Part 1 – Policies and products – Brian Fries – formerly Vice President, Project and Quality Management – Chemical Bank

Prior to its merger with Chase Manhattan Corporation, Chemical Banking Corporation was the fourth largest bank holding company in the USA employing over 40,000 staff in 35 countries and managing total assets of US$185 billion. The merger created the largest bank in the USA with assets of over US$300 billion.

For an organization of such scale, there are multiple potentially conflicting challenges. To ensure consistency and probity, it needs to maintain the highest possible levels of risk management and quality assurance. At the same time, the challenges of global competition and the demands of an ever more sophisticated client base put a tremendous emphasis on the needs for innovation, teamwork, empowerment and trust.

In the first of two chapters on Chemical's approach to managing innovation, Brian Fries presents the model used by Chemical Bank UK to define strategy, manage operations and implement change. He shows how the model is used to help analyse the environment, shape mission and vision and manage the changes required to deliver the strategy. Finally he describes Chemical's approaches to product innovation and quality management.

Chapter 7 – Managing innovation Part 2 – Processes – Brian Fries – formerly Vice President, Project and Quality Management – Chemical Bank

In the second of his two chapters, Brian Fries describes Chemical's approach to managing business processes and its methodology for running strategic change projects. He provides examples of how different elements of the process management approach have been applied to the processes for derivatives processing, risk management, product control, securities settlement, derivatives trading, treasury management and human resource management.

Finally, Brian describes how the project methodology was used to help manage the multiple streams of activity that took place as part of the merger of Chemical Bank and Chase Manhattan Bank.

Chapter 8 – Business transformation at MLC – An Australian Case Study – Oona Nielssen – Global Communications Manager – Lend Lease Property

In the MLC case, Oona Nielssen describes the employee driven transformation process in a once successful subsidiary of a major financial services institution which faced a stark choice of change or die in the face of increased competition and a rapidly changing marketplace.

MLC set itself the goal of achieving global best practice standards for financial institutions. The outcomes of this effort have been impressive. Over the period from December 1995 to December 1997 MLC achieved a fundamental change in culture and performance evidenced by its results. Most noticeable amongst these were a 25% increase in funds under management, a 51% productivity increase in funds under management per employee and a 19% reduction in costs.

A three pronged transformation process is described – the first involving simplification and rationalisation of the product portfolio. The second used a combination of accelerated 8-week Breakthrough programmes and larger scale Core Process Redesign initiatives to simplify business processes. The third element involved a highly participative approach that supported the creation of a learning-led, change adept culture. Finally Oona explains how the use of these techniques has now continued beyond the transformation process to become part of business as usual.

Chapter 9 – Using modern technology to build new capabilities – Clive Holtham – Bull Information Systems Professor of Information Management – City University Business School

Clive Holtham explores the strategic role of information technology (IT) in supporting organisational change. He argues that competitive advantage cannot be achieved simply through the purchase or application of IT. The real benefits, he suggests, only come when technology is combined with innovative actions and decisions regarding strategy, processes, people, information and organisation structures. Clearly, the developments in technology offer tremendous potential to those who can overcome the barriers to exploiting it successfully. Such developments also bring with them a new threat from competitors who have the technical capability to develop wholly new products and delivery methods.

The chapter starts with a discussion of some of the key models and frameworks used to illustrate the role of IT in organisational change. It then goes on to explore the challenges of managing 'legacy systems' and discusses the challenges of using IT to build new capabilities and 'change the rules of the game through IT'. Specific examples are provided of how IT is being exploited to create electronic cash, how the Internet is being used to create new delivery channels and how smaller banks can use the technology to facilitate collaboration and enable them to compete on a global scale.

Chapter 10 – Managing outsourcing and subcontracting – Edmond Cunningham – Principal Consultant – PA Consulting Group

Edmond Cunningham adopts Input Corporation's definition of Outsourcing as 'the long-term relationship (greater than one year) between a client and supplier in which the client delegates all, or a major portion, of a function to the supplier.' He argues that such an approach can help Financial Services firms respond competitively to changing customer needs. He suggests that for such a relationship to work, the firm must be clear on those activities which are 'core' to its future strategy. Only then can it set about identifying partners who can support it in the provision of 'non-core' activities.

The chapter introduces the concepts of outsourcing and the identification of core and non-core activities. The hard and soft factors that need to be considered in making the outsourcing decision are reviewed and the relationship between process redesign and outsourcing is discussed. Consideration is given to the critical challenges of preparing people, processes and systems for outsourcing, managing the transition, managing the contract and handling disputes. The role of consultants in the outsourcing process is examined and case studies are presented on the outsourcing experiences of The Co-operative Bank, Dunlop Aviation and Hill Samuel Life Assurance.

Chapter 11 – New era, new challenges, new strategies – Rohit Talwar

This chapter explores the challenges of competing in the Internet-enabled 21st century – in what many are describing as the New Economy. A brief overview is provided of some of the driving principles shaping the New Economy and the resulting implications for financial services are discussed. The change management implications of transforming to compete in the New Economy are considered. Finally, ideas are put forward on the basic components required of an infrastructure to support accelerated change.

Appendix – Resources for transformation and renewal – Rohit Talwar

A resource guide is presented highlighting websites, books, magazines and organisations that may prove useful sources of reference and inspiration to organisations embarking on transformation and renewal exercises.

CHAPTER ONE

Key management tools and techniques

Rohit Talwar, Director, FastFuture –
The Centre for Business
Transformation

A number of different tools and techniques are described in the chapters that follow. In this chapter I would like to explore two approaches referred to explicitly – the Balanced Business Scorecard and Business Process Re-engineering. I also felt it appropriate to explore the concept of participative approaches to change, which are implicit in many of the case studies.

Case studies are presented on the application of re-engineering and participation at Western Provident Association and TSB Bank.

The Balanced Business Scorecard

The concept of the Balanced Business Scorecard (BBS) developed by Kaplan and Norton[1] is structured to provide a balanced picture both of current business performance and of the factors which will determine future success. The aim is to encourage organizations to move from monitoring purely financial measures towards a more comprehensive framework that examines all the drivers of performance. The scorecard approach is also designed to help organizations consider the relationships between all the factors that influence results and use the resulting learning to drive continuous improvement.

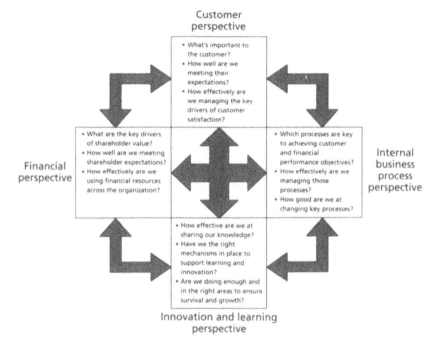

Fig. 1.1 Key perspectives and questions addressed by the Balanced Business Scorecard.

The BBS model is being adopted in numerous financial organizations including NatWest Group and Abbey National (Chapter 2). Numerous variations on the basic model have been developed, but most still focus on four interrelated perspectives (Fig. 1.1). The key benefits of such an approach are that it:

● Enables us to align departments, business units and resources to the organization's strategy;

● Forces us to consider the 'knock on' effects of changes made in any particular area;

● Provides greater clarity of the impact of operational changes on customer service and financial performance; and

● Encourages better informed and more balanced decision-making.

Business Process Re-engineering

Business Process Re-engineering (BPR) has been one of the most widely adopted management approaches over the last five years.

The term re-engineering was coined by Hammer and Champy[2] and defined as:

> the fundamental rethinking and redesign of business processes to achieve dramatic improvements in critical, contemporary measures of performance, such as cost, quality, service and speed.

The central principle of re-engineering is that we should look at our activities through the eyes of our customers. This implies looking at the end-to-end or 'horizontal' processes that cut across the different business functions and through which we provide service to both external and internal customers. Hence a process can be defined as:

> a sequence of activities performed on one or more inputs to deliver an output to the customer of the process.

Almost everything we do involves a process whether it be opening a new account, executing a transaction, conducting a staff appraisal or developing a new strategy. While many of our processes are documented and fully understood, there are a number where the 'design' is implicit – known only to those who execute the activity. The implicit nature of much process knowledge and the reluctance of people to share it are two of the biggest challenges that have to be overcome if a BPR exercise is to succeed.

Hence, when we talk about the difficulties of re-engineering business processes, we are really talking about the challenges of bringing about changes in people and cultures – subjects that are covered in considerable depth throughout this series. In practice, processes are what people engage in when they come to work, they are the way the organization delivers products and services to the customer and they are the main mechanism through which the organisation's culture manifests itself.

People are the critical element of any process. However if we consider Hammer and Champy's definition we find that they are not even mentioned. This is more than a passing observation – the most commonly cited cause of problems with BPR projects is failure to address the human and cultural dimensions. In contrast, the re-engineering success stories presented in this book all placed a heavy emphasis on the need for cultural change and the active involvement of staff in the redesign process. We will explore the nature of such participative approaches later in this chapter.

Indeed, rather than motivate people to rethink their processes, much of the language used by the likes of Hammer and Champy

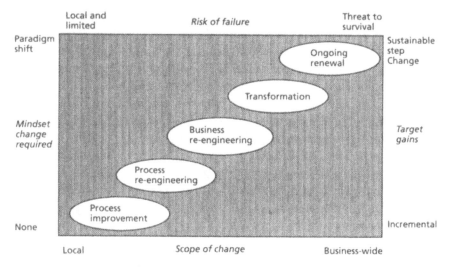

Fig. 1.2 The process change spectrum.

only served to increase the reluctance to participate. The literature is populated with suggestions that non-value adding tasks should be sought out and 'eliminated'. Similarly the recommendations for managing the change were that we should 'shoot the stragglers and carry the wounded'.

The problem is that the hype surrounding BPR often prevents meaningful discussions of what can be achieved. As we will see from the mini-cases in this chapter and from those in subsequent chapters, organizations have been able to use BPR to help bring about fundamental performance improvements and radically different ways of working.

Although the term re-engineering is used quite widely, it is clear that there is a wide range of interpretations of what it actually means. These are encapsulated in the process change spectrum (Fig. 1.2). Each of the approaches defined on the spectrum are valid ways of enhancing organizational performance. The challenge is to select an approach that will deliver the degree of change required by the organization's current situation.

Process improvement

This is the most common form of performance enhancement approach. It usually focuses on the part of a process that falls within a particular function rather than of the entire end to end process (e.g. the risk appraisal task performed by the underwriting department as part of the new business process that may start within the sales function). Whilst the improvements may centre on a process, this is not re-engineering in the truest sense of the word.

The emphasis in these initiatives is typically on improving rather than eliminating tasks. Such initiatives can take up to 3 months per process and yield improvements of 5–20% on key performance measures. Clearly, small changes to individual processes tend not to have a significant impact on bottom line business performance. However, the lessons from organizations undertaking Total Quality Management have shown that an organization-wide approach to process improvement can yield significant gains. The cases of Abbey National, Midland Bank and Chemical Bank highlight examples of successful approaches to continuous process improvement.

Process re-engineering

This involves the critical appraisal and redesign of an entire end to end process, e.g. developing a new product or processing an insurance claim. The typical duration is 3–15 months per process and the aim is to deliver improvements of 30% or more against critical measures of performance. Typical questions asked in such initiatives might include:

● What is the real added value for customers and what do they really want from the process?

● Why do we need to do this process in the first place?

● How would we run it if we were starting the business today?

● Would we pay for the tasks currently performed if we were the customer or shareholder?

Most process re-engineering initiatives require a combination of people, process, system, organization and communications changes. The approach should only be adopted if the gains cannot be achieved using less painful and demanding approaches. The results of successful initiatives can have a significant impact on overall business performance. In Chapter 5 we hear how Britannia Building Society used process re-engineering to bring about dramatic improvements in the process of collecting mortgage arrears.

Business re-engineering

This is a logical next step from process re-engineering in which firms seek to achieve step change improvements across all or most of their customer facing and internal processes. Such far-reaching changes usually place a much greater spotlight on the overall design or 'architecture' of the business. Organizational structure may well be realigned to ensure that form (i.e. functions and hierarchies) follows content (customer facing processes).

Such initiatives usually last anything from 12 to 36 months and critical success measures would be the impact on bottom line performance and the sustainability of the gains. The cases of Western Provident Association (Box 1.1) and TSB Bank (Box 1.2) highlight the benefits that can be achieved through such all-encompassing programmes of process change.

Transformation

Some organizations are attempting to apply re-engineering as part of an overall process of 'reinventing the business'. Such initiatives typically start by questioning the organization's purpose, values and goals. Only then do they go on to look at how work is organized in order to achieve those goals. Hence, the initial planning investment tends to be significantly higher than for the other change approaches. Often – as in the case of Mortgage Express described in Chapter 4 – the transformation is undertaken in response to a crisis.

A number of firms would claim to have undergone a successful transformation. The tests of whether a transformation had actually occurred would include:

- Step change improvements against all critical measures/benchmarks of business performance.

- The perception amongst staff that the business is a dramatically better place to work in than 3–5 years ago.

- A belief amongst customers, suppliers and other business partners that the organization has become far easier and far better to work with and has helped them save time and cost.

- Organization-wide clarity of purpose, direction, business architecture and capabilities.

Box 1.1 Business Re-engineering at Western Provident Association

WPA – history

Western Provident Association (WPA) is a UK provider of private health insurance. Established in 1938 as the Bristol Hospitals Fund it was renamed as WPA in 1949. Whilst the organization had achieved steady growth its administration had remained largely unchanged until the appointment of Julian Stainton as Chief Executive in 1987.

The starting point for change

On his arrival, Stainton found that he had inherited a 1950s style business that was losing staff and customers 'at an alarming rate'. 370 customer facing staff were employed to handle 400,000 customers whose details were held in over 1 million paper files. The business was supported by one computer, one desktop PC and four telephone lines that were disconnected in the afternoons to enable staff to get on with their work.

Stainton found that the business was receiving an average of 50 complaints per day. Demotivated staff were hiding the most difficult customer case files and sabotaging telephones to prevent them from ringing. A first examination of the core processes revealed that a typical claim passed through seven departments before being settled.

The change process

Convinced that change was essential, Stainton set about the transformation of WPA. At the heart of the change process were three key factors:

● Energetic and committed leadership from Stainton.

● Investment in and involvement of staff.

● An intolerance of underperformance.

A new vision, mission and values statement was produced following extensive staff consultation and a general philosophy was adopted of organizing WPA around the needs of its customers. A target was set of achieving industry-best service and major investments were made in staff training and two-way communications. The business was relocated from Bristol to a purpose-built site in Taunton.

The business was restructured into seven self-managing departments each servicing a different customer group and each responsible for its own targets, budgets, staffing and procurement. To ensure high levels of service and flexibility, the departments were set up as multi-skilled customer oriented work teams modelled on the Volvo production model. These were underpinned by the creation of key technical and support departments. The processes themselves were streamlined with many now being executed by a single case worker performing the entire end-to-end process. At the same time most inter-departmental communications posts were eliminated.

The redesign of core processes was supported by a heavy investment in IT bringing in document image processing, open systems and a client server architecture. In order to ensure effective support to the business, IT staff are required to spend one-third of their time working in the business. Systems are developed using a highly participative rapid application development approach. Over 25% of the staff have now been involved in prototyping new systems. As a result of the systems investment, all staff have access to customer correspondence and the enquiry system. The general philosophy is to exploit technology to help move the business towards a paperless environment.

Whilst many of the staff readily embraced and engaged in the change process it was not universally accepted. Staff were asked to apply for the re-engineered posts and those that didn't left voluntarily. Of the 35 managers in post when Stainton arrived, only one chose to stay on in the re-engineered organization.

The results of change – service improvement

As a result of re-engineering, the new business processing cycle has been reduced from 7 people doing 45 minutes work over 28 days to 1 person doing 4 minutes work in less than 4 days. Overall the business has seen a 30% service improvement and a 100% increase in productivity. In Stainton's words, the technology infrastructure now provides 'everything you ever wanted to know about your customer available to everyone who needs to know it'. All incoming calls are answered in three rings.

Complaints were reduced to 12 in 1995 whilst 200 letters of thanks were received. Every complainant receives a personal visit from a WPA director to investigate the problem. No customer claims are contested – and WPA is achieving a 99.5% success rate against its guarantee of settlement in seven days. The business has received numerous awards and acknowledgements of its performance and has won NOP/Gallup service awards for three years running.

Business impact

The number of customer facing staff has been reduced from 360 to 150 – for whom salaries have gone up 8% in real terms over the last 3 years. Absenteeism is running at approximately 1% which is one-third of the national average. Renewal rates are up to 95% and the business achieved 14.4% customer growth in 1995 against a general market decline. As a result, WPA now has over 600,000 customers. Income rose to over £100M in 1996 from c£40M in 1987 and reserves were up from £13M in 1987 to £54M.

Next steps

Despite the remarkable success achieved by WPA, Julian Stainton believes the biggest threat is complacency. As a result the organization is embarking on a new round of changes designed to make greater use of existing organizational knowledge to improve efficiency and the quality of service to customers.

Clearly, the re-engineering of core business processes will be a critical component of an organizational transformation. However, the emphasis on processes should not be allowed to detract from the more fundamental challenges of affecting a transformation. In the vast majority of current transformation initiatives, re-engineering is the start point or catalyst for the larger transformation. In the latter case, the organization may have started out with more humble aims but then recognised that the desired gains can only be achieved by a complete transformation.

Box 1.2 BPR in TSB – 'hearts and minds'

by Ron J. Whatford, Managing Director, Central Operations, Lloyds TSB Group plc

In order to re-engineer the processes within TSB, it was first necessary to introduce a new way of thinking. The concepts of processes and process management do not traditionally sit easily within financial service organizations. This is in contrast to the manufacturing industry, where the concepts of the flow of work and process control are commonplace. This is easy to understand, given that waste in manufacturing is very obvious. A company making radiator grilles which do not fit the body shells of the cars for which the grille was made, will very quickly identify the problem, and the failure of the process is there for all to see.

Make failures visible

In financial services, however, it is much more difficult to bring to light errors, rework and rejects caused by the failure of business processes. Traditionally, the situation has been dealt with either by throwing people at the problem, or by creatively coping thereby putting another loop in the process. Neither of these approaches deals with the removal of the root cause of the non-conformance, or eliminate the failure once and for all. This is particularly so when work is viewed in a department or section context and it is possible for one department to improve its own performance at the expense of another department, as well as to the detriment of the overall performance of the end to end process.

The need to make process failures visible in the organization was recognised at TSB, and we first set out to win the hearts and minds of the people involved in order to radically improve the company's customer service and cost performance. The company already had the advantage of having carried out a TQM training programme – which extended to all the staff in the retail bank – led by the TSB Group Chief Executive, Peter Ellwood. In this way, we had already created an environment in which we could set about mapping and measuring our key business processes.

Winning hearts and minds

The process of winning and retaining hearts and minds had to begin with building undeniable cases for the proposed changes which would create the necessary emotional appeal for the programme as a whole. This involved identifying and viewing work from an end to end process perspective, i.e. from customer need to customer satisfaction, using comprehensive research from customers to ensure that priority was given to those areas of our performance which were most important to the customer. This strategy of illustrating 'rogue' processes (those processes which failed to deliver the required level of service and carried unnecessary costs) was a critical part of the first stages of building the momentum for change. This approach of centring on the whole process, in the name of the customer, enabled the focus to shift away from blaming specific individuals and on to process deficiency. This focus was made more sharp by building into the description of the 'rogue' process a statement of the proportion of time when value was being added, as a percentage of the time taken to complete the process.

The customers' perspective

Having created the case for change, work then commenced on developing views of how these processes should ideally work for the benefit of customers, in order

---

to meet their needs now and, more especially, in the future. Much work was undertaken in identifying potential external threats and in developing alternative scenarios in support of this objective. Critically, this involved staff from across the organization participating in and contributing to the change programme. This participation was taken forward through the establishment of process teams whose role was to champion local process improvements and spread the language and concept of process right across the organization, as well as supporting a programme of radical improvement activity, specifically targeted at key customer-facing processes.

Cross-functional teams
For many people working in these cross-functional teams, developing the process perspective proved a powerful and rewarding experience. Nonetheless, considerable effort was expended in reinforcing the need for change through the use of presentations, external examples, lobbying, and debate, especially with the few dissenters who remained. Together with the continual visible support from senior management, the hearts and minds of staff in TSB were quickly won over and for the very small minority of dissenters who remained, agreement to disagree was accepted as reasonable. In this way, the progress of the programme was not hampered, and the creation of 'programme terrorists' was prevented.

'Quick wins'
The overall programme has now been embedded within the company business plan, and successes have been publicised in the company magazine, highlighting particularly those quick wins which local management have achieved, and which were so critical to obtaining and retaining the longer term funding and commitment required, in what is a radical change programme.

The pay-off
At TSB, there has always been a strong commitment to customer service and meeting the needs of the individual throughout the entire company, but most noticeably in the minds of staff dealing with customers on a day-to-day basis. Linking the radical change programme to a customer perspective, and viewing the processes as they affect the customer, has enabled the company to harness the underlying commitment of staff across the organization, and deliver significant change – to the benefit of customers, staff, and shareholders.

Ongoing renewal

Even if the organization has undergone a successful transformation the process does not end there. The techniques used and the new ways of thinking that have developed must be embedded in the organization's culture and methods of working so that it can continue to refocus and reinvent itself in line with changes in its commercial environment.

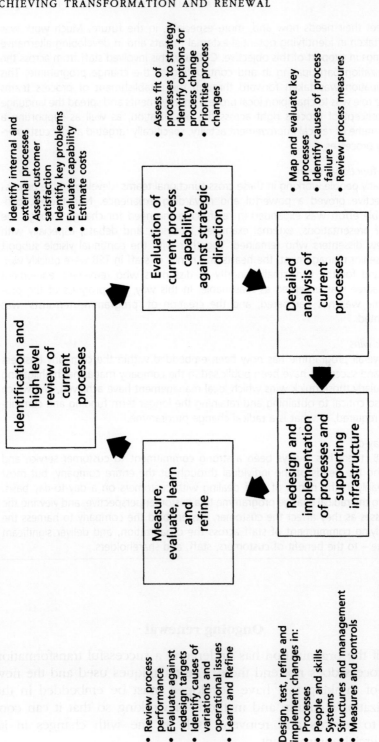

- Identify internal and external processes
- Assess customer satisfaction
- Identify key problems
- Evaluate capability
- Estimate costs

- Assess fit of processes to strategy
- Identify options for process change
- Prioritise process changes

Evaluation of current process capability against strategic direction

Identification and high level review of current processes

- Map and evaluate key processes
- Identify causes of process failure
- Review process measures

Detailed analysis of current processes

Measure, evaluate, learn and refine

Redesign and implementation of processes and supporting infrastructure

- Review process performance
- Evaluate against redesign targets
- Identify causes of variations and operational issues
- Learn and Refine

Design, test, refine and implement changes in:
- Processes
- People and skills
- Systems
- Structures and management
- Measures and controls

Fig. 1.3 A framework for process review and re-engineering.

Re-engineering approaches

Re-engineering methods and approaches have been refined considerably over the past few years. Greater emphasis is now being placed on the need for early involvement – as in the cases of TSB and Mortgage Express. There is also a growing awareness of the need to capture and act on the learning that results from conducting a process change initiative. The framework presented in Fig. 1.3 shows how learning can be incorporated as a formal element in the re-engineering process.

It is the need to encourage and accelerate organizational learning that has led many organizations to adopt a more participative approach to change. The thinking behind this approach is described below.

Participative approaches to change

The need for new approaches to change

Despite the tremendous successes achieved by the organizations discussed here, all would acknowledge that the process of change has been difficult and continues to present new challenges. One of the most frequently voiced concerns is that whilst re-engineering may speed up the execution of core tasks the change process itself remains unacceptably slow. A second concern is that many re-engineered solutions rely on greater empowerment and responsibility for staff. Where such changes have been imposed there is a natural contradiction between the way in which change is delivered and the desired outcomes.

Another problem lies in the way change is designed and conducted. Typically a small project team is formed to analyse the situation and develop recommendations. Frequently the team finds that it can be well into its task but the goals and terms of reference for the initiative have still to be agreed by all of the key stakeholders. Furthermore, because of the difficulties of bringing the key stakeholders together at a single point in time, the project team is left with the unenviable task of integrating multiple potentially conflicting viewpoints.

Furthermore, with the ever-increasing pace of change in most organizations, the project team often has incomplete knowledge about critical factors that may affect their work. Those with the knowledge may not even be aware that the project team exists. Furthermore, the observation and interview based process review methods used by project teams often fail to surface many of the real operational issues and concerns of those working on the front line.

The attraction of participative approaches

As a result of their frustrations, many organizations such as Mortgage Express, MLC, TSB and Western Provident Association are turning to more participative approaches to change. Participative approaches start with the premise that however compelling the case for change, however radical and potentially beneficial the proposed solutions, the actual implementation of change rarely succeeds unless it is owned and delivered by the front line managers and staff. Indeed it is they who are typically left to resolve the post-implementation issues created by poorly designed change initiatives.

The mechanics of participation

Participation seeks to bring together focused groups of 5–100 people using a range of intensive, fixed timescale activities. Larger gatherings are not uncommon. For example, during its transformation programme, the South African Ministry of Water Affairs[3] held open-air events involving up to 5,000 people. Whatever their size, participative events are typically aimed at addressing specific organizational challenges from defining a new vision to redesigning the new product development process. A key to the success of these sessions is to ensure that 'the whole system is in the room' (Fig. 1.4), i.e. all – or as many as possible – of those who have an interest or influence on the outcome are bought together to resolve the issue at one time. It is also important that the scope of the issue and boundaries are clearly established beforehand.

Whilst much of the design and decision making is done in the event, the fine tuning and detailed implementation planning and preparation is done 'in the field'. These 'events' are typically supported by extensive communication between the workshop participants and the communities they represent. Increasingly organizations such as TSB are using quality action teams or local

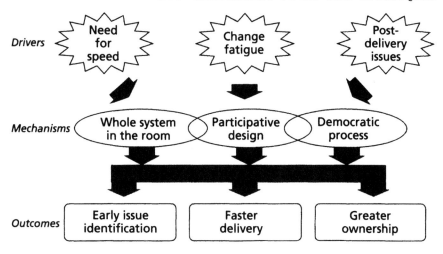

Fig. 1.4 Principles of participative approaches.

improvement teams to follow through on decisions made in the workshops.

Participative approaches acknowledge that today's problems are frequently yesterday's solutions, and that we need a broad range of stakeholder perspectives if we are to understand the causes of failure and fully appreciate future requirements. Hence during participative sessions all voices are considered equal and participants work together to review the past, understand the present and define and design the future.

Because of the clear focus on outcomes, shared learning, speed and co-operation, participative events provide real, hands on experience of the culture and working disciplines many organizations are keen to develop throughout their organizations. Finally, by using the participants as the main medium of communication throughout, participation ensures that real issues and concerns are addressed early in the change process.

In practice, participative approaches are generally adopted by organizations that are feeling a sense of frustration with traditional approaches that deliver great ideas but little practical change. The main drawback is that it requires key people to come together and resolve issues within a compressed timescale. However, experience from the case study organizations suggests that resistance to participation generally diminishes rapidly once the first such event takes place and the results become visible.

The underlying principles

The underlying premise is that people generally feel 'ownership' for that which they create, hence if we want front line staff to understand and own the 'design for change' they must be involved in the design process. The more we engage the front line in the design process, the more likely we are to identify and address the real issues that traditional analytical approaches may not surface or challenge.

For example, when Birmingham Midshires Building Society – winners of the 1996 Management Today Service Excellence award – embarked on its latest round of process changes, over 300 people volunteered to be involved in the development of a new computer system. Despite the logistical challenges this presented, all were accommodated within different aspects of the project and helped to ensure rapid delivery of a high quality system.

Once we have understanding, ownership and participation we have the conditions in which trust is created and empowerment can succeed. Bringing different parts of the organization together to view issues from multiple perspectives and experiment with new ideas and approaches helps to unleash and harness the latent talent and intellectual, physical and emotional energy that lies unused in many organizations.

Whilst by no means a universal panacea, the attraction of participative approaches are that they can deliver comprehensive solutions quickly – cutting traditional change cycles by 50–80%.

References

1. Glaser, P., Hobbs, S., Johnson, C. and Moema, D. *The Design and Facilitation of a transformational Intiative in the South African National Department of Water Affairs and Forestry* presentation to fifth Ecology of Work Conference, Dublin 15th May 1997.
2. Hammer, Michael and Champy James *Reengineering the Corporation – A Manifesto for Business Revolution,* Nicholas Brealey Publishing, 1993.
3. Jackson, M. – Chief Executive Birmingham Midshires Building Society *Beyond Re-engineering* presentation to UK Strategic Planning Society Re-engineering and Radical Change Special Interest Group April 16th 1996.
4. Kaplan, R. S. and Norton, D. P. *The Balanced Scorecard – Translating Strategy into Action* 1996.

Reference sources for Western Provident Association Case Study (Box 1.1):

Courtney, N. *Case Study: Western Provident Association Ltd.* City University Business School Case Study 1994

Site visit by the author on March 14th 1997

Stainton, J. Chief Executive – Western Provident Association *Building a Knowledge Based Organisation* presentation to UK Strategic Planning Society Re-engineering and Radical Change Special Interest Group March 24th 1997

Further reading

Davenport, Thomas *Process Innovation* (1993) Harvard Business School Press

Hammer, Michael 'Reengineering Work – Don't Automate Obliterate', *Harvard Business Review* July–Aug 1990

Pascale, R. et al. 'Riding the Reinvention Rollercoaster' *Harvard Business Review* Nov–Dec 1993

Scott-Morton, M. (Ed) *The Corporation of the 1990s* OUP 1991

Semler, Ricardo *Maverick* (1993) Century Press

Senge Peter et al. *The Fifth Discipline Fieldbook* (1994) Nicholas Brealey Publishing

Talwar, Rohit '*Business Reengineering – A Strategy Driven Approach,*' *Long Range Planning*, Vol 26 – 6 December 1993

Talwar, Rohit '*Reengineering – A Wonderdrug for the 90s*', in *Business Process Reengineering: Myth & Reality*, ed: Coulson-Thomas C., Kogan Page, (September 1994)

CHAPTER TWO

Managing change at Abbey National

Tim Murley, Director, Strategic Performance Improvement, Abbey National

Introduction

Abbey National has managed its share of change in the past decade. Perhaps the largest and best known change came in 1989, when we became the first building society to convert to plc status. But other major changes have punctuated our recent history as well. In 1983 we led the break-up of the building societies cartel. And following our conversion to plc status, we launched our treasury operations – Abbey National Treasury Services plc – the wholesale banking arm of the company. Subsequently, we embarked upon an expansion into the bancassurance field, first by acquiring Scottish Mutual in 1992 and then by establishing Abbey National Life in 1993. In 1995, we continued to expand our range of services by launching Abbey National General Insurance (ANGI), a joint venture with Commercial Union, and by acquiring First National Finance Corporation, the UK's leading provider of point of sale consumer credit. And in 1996 the whole of the National & Provincial Building Society's business was transferred to Abbey National.

The company now consists of four main businesses: UK Retail Banking, Insurance, Treasury & Offshore and Consumer Credit.

Diversification – which we feel is necessary to remain competitive in an increasingly challenging business environment – will continue to be a driver of change for Abbey National.

Improved technology, combined with an increased willingness on the part of the public to use it, has also been a catalyst of change within the financial services sector – including, for example, the growth of telephone sales. Launches of direct marketing operations by other financial services providers attracted a good deal of press attention in the mid-90s, but Abbey National had been selling mortgages by phone since 1989. We are not afraid to be innovative, and we have often been leaders in change.

Change in moderation

Those major events notwithstanding, Abbey National is not a company that engages in change for change's sake. We are not a company that undertakes radical restructuring in the hope of getting some good press coverage or winning over a few customers from a rival bank. We do not follow the 'Big Bang' approach to change – attempting to 'turn things around overnight'.

Perhaps that is because we haven't needed to. By most accounts, Abbey National has been extremely successful in navigating a changing industry. From first being quoted on the Stock Exchange in

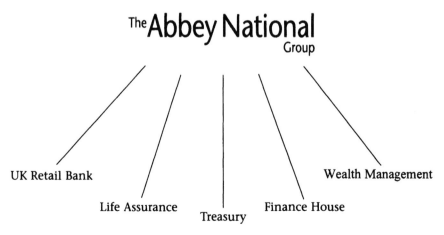

Fig. 2.1 The business areas of Abbey National.

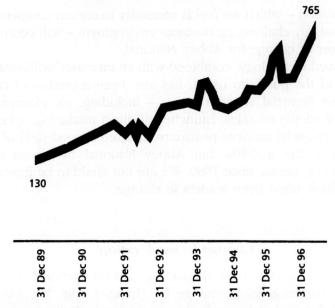

765

130

31 Dec 89
31 Dec 90
31 Dec 91
31 Dec 92
31 Dec 93
31 Dec 94
31 Dec 95
31 Dec 96

Fig. 2.2 Abbey National share price from flotation, 11 July 1989 to 31 December 1996.

July 1989 to the end of 1996, Abbey National's share price increased from 130p to 765p, with shareholder dividends increasing year-on-year. During the period 1990 to 1996, our total shareholder return – reflecting share price increases plus gross dividends – was more than 28 per cent per annum. This ranked us second in the FT-SE 100.

When Abbey National converted to plc status, about five million people became shareholders, many for the first time. Indeed, Abbey National's conversion increased the total number of private shareholders in the UK from six million to nine and a half million. We essentially changed the complexion of share ownership in the UK.

What happened at the same time was a blurring of the boundary between shareholders and customers. At the time of our conversion, these two groups were nearly identical. Even in 1997, more than six years after conversion, over 2 million of our 2.5 million shareholders were also customers.

It is little surprise, therefore, that we have adopted a corporate strategy that places great emphasis on the growth of shareholder value.

Value-based management

In Abbey National's most recent mission statement, developed in 1994, we set out the company's underlying purpose: to achieve above-average growth in shareholder value over the long term. Indeed, Abbey National shareholders have enjoyed total returns among the best in the FT-SE 100. But we cannot assume that this trend will automatically continue.

As a result, value-based management (VBM) plays an important role in our corporate planning and strategy process at the highest level. Briefly put, VBM dictates that the central driving force behind our management decisions is the creation of value for our shareholders. There are numerous manifestations of this approach – including an emphasis on the effective use of capital and a focus on post-tax, rather than pre-tax, profits – but the thrust of it is that it places primary importance on the perspective of our investors.

Balanced Business Scorecard

Taking into consideration the importance of VBM, and given the complexity of a large and diversifying company, Abbey National saw the need to develop a means for measuring the company's health in a more comprehensive way.

At the same time, we wanted to focus on non-financial measures as well as financial ones. VBM points us toward assessing the company's progress in terms of financial measures – most prominently, share price and dividends – but non-financial measures directly impact on the financial ones. To produce financial results that satisfy shareholders, the company must deliver outstanding service to customers through a well-trained and motivated staff – goals that cannot always be measured in financial terms.

As a result, we have adopted and implemented the Balanced Business Scorecard, an approach to measuring performance that draws from four central perspectives:

- customers;
- innovation and improvement;
- internal processes;
- traditional financial measurements.

Within each of these four areas is a set of key performance indicators (KPIs), which reflect specific, measurable activities. In

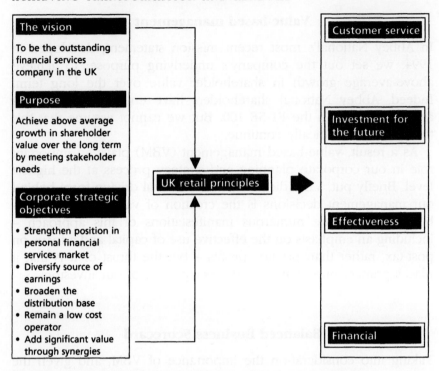

Fig. 2.3 Abbey National: UK retail Balanced Business Scorecard.

Abbey National's scorecard, there are a total of thirty-four KPIs, ranging from 'Customer satisfaction' to 'Employee motivation' to 'Profit after capital charge'. In Abbey National's balanced scorecard, each KPI has a 'Lead owner' – an executive director who reports on the performance of the area to the Chief Executive – and a 'Contact' – a manager who is directly responsible for the development and accuracy of the figures.

The Balanced Business Scorecard is a flexible tool that can be adapted to the specific goals and activities of a given company. The principle remains the same for all who use it: that the scorecard should assess the company from diverse perspectives, all being broken down into specific measurable units which are all linked, whether directly or indirectly, with the company's overall goal – in Abbey National's case, to increase shareholder value.

Several examples will illustrate how these non-financial measures reflect the health of the company.

The key performance indicator of 'Employee turnover' – which is 'owned' by the Human Resources Director – measures the number of leavers as an annualized percentage of the total headcount. The result gives an indication of staff motivation and is an early indicator of recruitment training costs.

'Customer satisfaction', a KPI in the purview of the Managing Director Retail Division, provides a numerical score that reflects responses to customer surveys about Abbey National's services. It measures Abbey National's customers' perceptions of the company in terms of reliability, accuracy, responsiveness, and other standards.

One KPI that measures the quality of service from an operational point of view is 'Service Standards', which is overseen by the Managing Director Retail Division. This KPI reflects the percentage of services provided that are within the Abbey National standard. It shows how often we meet our service goals – for example, processing an application within a given time-frame. This information is cross-matched with customer satisfaction figures to indicate whether gaps are caused by changes in actual performance or by changing expectations.

Overall, the scorecard has proved to be a valuable management tool in providing a balanced view of the company from the perspectives of different stakeholders. It provides both financial and non-financial information necessary to establish and follow corporate strategy. It ensures balance in reporting among all interests and helps guide progress towards the corporate strategic direction.

Accordingly, the Balanced Business Scorecard is a necessary instrument in managing change. More than simply a measurement tool, it provides information on a range of leading and lagging indicators, and as such it provides managers valuable information for evaluating the current position of the company and for managing future progress.

Strategic Performance Improvement

Actually implementing change requires a facilitator, someone who can say how to get from here to there. Strategic Performance Improvement (SPI) is the entity within Abbey National that provides consulting services to other departments wishing to implement change.

Positioned within Abbey National's HR Division, SPI supports the efforts of departments throughout the Group to improve performance. SPI's stated mission is 'to support the business in becoming the outstanding financial services company in the UK by assisting

ACHIEVING TRANSFORMATION AND RENEWAL

managers in the development and execution of programmes to improve customer service and cost effectiveness.' In this endeavour to produce focused change, the Balanced Business Scorecard proves invaluable.

SPI aims to provide a source of expertise in helping the company examine and measure its own business performance. Then, through the application of structured techniques, we help our 'clients' (the departments within Abbey National for whom we work) develop appropriate solutions to their business problems.

SPI's standard procedure includes five steps:

● *Initiation* – to understand the customer's needs and to define the purpose, scope, and objectives of the review. At this stage, we produce a 'project charter', effectively a contract between SPI and the department for whom we are conducting the review.

● *Data collection* – to capture sufficient data and information to establish an effective approach to the problem and to enable an accurate analysis.

● *Analysis* – to analyse the information and identify variations, causes, and ideal requirements.

● *Options development* – to evaluate options for change based on the analysis and to develop recommendations.

● *Implementation planning* – to prepare a broad implementation plan so that all parties are aware of their responsibilities and are committed to progressing.

This last stage, as well as the first stage, highlights the need for all performance improvement projects to enjoy adequate sponsorship. Each project must be fully supported at all levels; it must be 'sponsored' by an executive manager, and the line managers must effectively 'own' the project.

At Abbey National, we aim to minimize the company's use of external consultants, thereby controlling the cost of acquiring new methodologies, tools and techniques. If we can perform a project solely with in-house resources, we will. However, if we do need to hire outside consultants, we will hire them for specific skills. And to ensure that the value of the consultancy is retained, we will require that the consultants transfer those skills to appropriate Abbey National personnel.

As discussed earlier, Abbey National is not a company that goes for the 'Big Bang' approach to change. Rather, the company advocates implementing projects of varied size.

Fig. 2.4 Performance improvement methodologies.

We have found that projects can be plotted against two variables: return and time/risk. Logically, the higher the return desired, the higher the time and risk required. At the low end of both scales is overhead cost management. All businesses must practise this; it is the regular monitoring and control of costs. At the other end of the spectrum, however, is business process re-engineering. This is the complete reworking of a major process. Although Abbey National does undertake projects of this magnitude, SPI's role is to ensure that the company manages change through a mixture of high-risk to low-risk projects.

Leadership and change

We recognize that managing change is not simply a matter of conducting a study, developing recommendations, and implementing them. Managing change must take into consideration the people who are affected.

We operate under the assumption that people are not opposed to change in itself. After all, many people put a great deal of energy into initiating changes such as job promotions, pay increases, and improved working conditions. People do, however, react negatively to change where they perceive that it will result in a loss of their status, skill, or job satisfaction. Managing change successfully requires dealing with any perception of loss.

Moreover, any change is likely to produce some degree of resistance. In fact, we have found that the response to change is characterized by the progression through four stages:

1. denial;

2. resistance;

3. exploration;

4. commitment.

To promote a high level of performance, our goal is to support and encourage staff to move swiftly from the negative stages – denial and resistance – to the positive stages – exploration and commitment. This requires leadership from all levels of management. During the first two stages, managers must explain the changes and listen to and empathize with the anger, concern, apathy and withdrawal the staff display. And during the latter two stages, managers must encourage staff to participate in an active learning process so that issues can be confronted, solutions found, and a new future defined. Accordingly, we must help managers gain the skills to move staff through this entire process.

Case studies

In supporting the efforts of various departments within Abbey National to implement change, SPI utilizes various methods of measuring business performance. The first two case studies presented here, benchmarking and activity-based costing, examine the development of two measurement techniques that have proven valuable in Abbey National's management of change. The remainder of these case studies – examining the branch best practice, procurement and quality service reviews – show how we have successfully moved from the identification and measurement of a problem through to implementation.

Benchmarking

World-wide surveys indicate that well over two-thirds of leading companies are conducting benchmarking on a regular basis. Furthermore, almost all of them expect to increase their investment in benchmarking over the next five years, thus confirming that benchmarking will be a key management technique of the 90s and beyond.

Benchmarking is an ongoing learning experience. It identifies and evaluates practices and performance, allowing an organization to increase its effectiveness, efficiency, profitability and adaptability. It also provides a systematic way to identify superior products, services, processes and practices that can be adopted or adapted to your own environment to reduce costs, enhance customer service and generally become more competitive.

Benchmarking is not just a question of comparing one organization to another; it involves identifying opportunities for improvement and initiating change.

Using benchmarking at Abbey National

Abbey National has made benchmarking a significant part of its corporate strategy. Through benchmarking, we aim to:

- improve service to the customer;
- identify best practices;
- improve allocation of resources;
- increase efficiency.

Abbey National requires support and input from a number of sources before commencing a benchmarking initiative:

- *Sponsor*: an executive-level sponsor who can agree overall strategy and support the active use of benchmarking results to achieve real change in the organization.
- *Driver*: to attend regular meetings, make executive decisions on the benchmarking initiative, propose changes in strategy and agree tactical plans.
- *Data manager*: arguably the most important role, responsible on a day-to-day basis for assuring the quality of the benchmarking information being provided by their organization.

Initiatives and results

Abbey National has participated in a number of benchmarking initiatives, gathering information on:

- the mortgage process;
- the retail savings process;
- unsecured credit risk management;
- telephone services;
- bancassurance.

Significant changes can emerge from benchmarking studies. For example, Abbey National embarked on a benchmarking programme in the early 1990s to see how cost efficient we were in processing mortgages. The programme, co-ordinated by Coopers & Lybrand, gathered data from several major banks and building societies. Through the benchmarking study, which continues to give us quarterly reports, we have been able to measure aspects such as the unit cost of processing, the handling time, and the elapsed time of the entire process. As a direct result of the data gathered, we identified areas where duplication of effort was occurring which was above the average levels for other companies. As a result, we studied the problem in-depth and applied best practice methodologies to devise a solution. The end result was an improvement in the efficiency of our mortgage processing – a measurable change.

Of course, there are difficulties inherent in implementing benchmarking initiatives and making sure they actually work. All too often, they show results that we don't want to see. They reveal bad news. So if a company is not prepared to accept that bad news, the benchmarking effort is pointless.

In addition, benchmarking projects are especially difficult ones to manage internally, with formidable challenges in ensuring that managers who will be involved in implementing change are made a part of the process. It is crucial to ensure that staff are kept fully involved, so that they can become facilitators of change.

The end result is paramount; for benchmarking to be effective, it must be integrated with the planning and strategy formulation process, and then used to make change happen.

Activity-based costing

While benchmarking drives change by providing information obtained outside the company, information must also come from within. The formation of Abbey National's management information strategy in 1993 advocated the use of activity-based costing (ABC) as a valuable source of internal information about the company's financial performance.

Activity-based costing aims to allow managers to examine the costs of an activity and of what drives that activity. It gives managers a better idea of what they are spending and why.

Unlike traditional accounting measures, ABC allows an organization to determine the costs associated with a specific activity throughout the entire company – costs that include input from the branch network, marketing, technology support and finance.

Developing ABC at Abbey National

Abbey National's decision to undertake an activity-based costing initiative was driven by several main factors, including:

● the recognition that existing information did not help us understand the implications of business decisions or to measure performance;

● the need to better understand both costs and revenues for our products and customers;

● the need to identify and address inefficient processes and activities;

● the recognition that we need to improve the way in which we undertake the budget process.

As a tool for measuring the costs and benefits of a variety of activities, ABC helps to create a framework for change: identifying areas for improvement and measuring progress towards set goals.

Implementation

To evaluate the contribution that ABC could make to the company, Abbey National implemented a pilot project. With the help of Price Waterhouse, we developed a methodology that could be used for future ABC reviews examining other areas of the business. The pilot project addressed the Instant Saver Account, an existing Abbey National product, and through the project we were able to use ABC to segment the customer base – looking at variables such as the level of balance kept in the account and the number of transactions.

In subsequent implementations of ABC, we have found the method to play a valuable role in the decision-making process. However, we expect this role to expand. More specifically, we expect ABC to be increasingly used in:

● product analysis – determining costs involved in bringing products to market;

● customer analysis – providing information for customer relationship management, which can be used, for example, to determine customer profitability;

- process analysis – determining costs attributable to identified processes in, for example, delivering customer service;

- supply chain analysis – analysing the costs of supplying commodities such as cash;

- benchmarking – identifying opportunities to increase efficiency;

- Balanced Business Scorecard – measuring progress;

- planning and budgeting – setting targets; and

- continuous improvement.

The effort to develop our ABC methods and to implement ABC over a broad range of the company's areas has yielded some broader benefits, as well. Primarily, it has pointed to the need for an integrated and focused management information strategy, one that would support the commitment to profit improvement initiatives and would help us better understand the potential impact of business decisions on shareholder value.

As a measurement technique, it feeds information into the Balanced Business Scorecard and serves as an important initiator of change.

Branch best practice

The competitive market in UK retail banking requires financial services providers to continually strive to improve business performance without increasing resources. This is a stated strategic objective of Abbey National – to remain a low-cost operator.

Project objectives

Achieving this goal requires that we maximize our potential within the retail branch network. A logical step towards those objectives was Abbey National's Branch Best Practice Review, initiated in 1994. The review sought to improve the performance of our branch network, which consists of outlets throughout the UK.

We had found that there was considerable variation in the performance of these branches, largely the result of differing working practices. We recognized, furthermore, that these variations offered an opportunity to improve the ability of the branches to:

- meet customer needs;
- increase sales performance;
- improve cost effectiveness.

Accordingly, the best practice approach had the goal of identifying the best individual practices among our network of branches and to establish guidelines that could be used to improve the performance across the network.

Best practice methodology

The project adopted a methodology developed jointly between Ernst and Young and Abbey National's Strategic Performance Improvement unit. The methodology was based on a recognized and well-proven approach, but tailored to Abbey National's organizational standards. The resulting methodology, to which Abbey National owns the intellectual property rights, has been applied to best practice reviews of several areas of the company:

- the mortgage application process;
- the Financial Planning Service, which sells comprehensive financial planning services as well as regulated products;
- staff and workloads management;
- the company's business development units, which sell mortgages through our introducers.

Typical of these projects, the best practice reviews of the mortgage application process progressed through the following stages.

- The first stage was to document existing practices. We sought to find out what actually happens at key stages in the mortgage application process.

- Next, we determined measures that could be used to evaluate performance. We asked: What are the variables that contribute towards quality service in the mortgage application process, and how can they be measured?

- Having determined what it was we were looking for, we visited a representative sample of branches and collected data on performance.

- After analysing the data, we visited branches that appeared to be either high or low performers and conducted detailed structured interviews at all levels of staff. Our goal here was to define more carefully the practices being followed and to identify the causes for the branches' performance.

Having drawn conclusions about effective practices, we formulated recommendations and communicated our findings back to the branches. This involved producing a handbook of guidelines and conducting face-to-face briefings to branch representatives.

The representatives conveyed the information to all staff in the branches and also relayed to head office feedback received from branch employees. The use of these representatives (dubbed 'champions') was not just one-off; they have continued to be used to evaluate the implementation and success of our best practice guidelines on an ongoing basis.

Outcomes

The work carried out in the review of mortgage application process confirmed that a there was a wide range in the levels of performance at different branches. Although many of the practices were indeed simple or common sense, they were not used across the network.

So what the best practice review accomplished was to provide guidelines to practices that could be used throughout the branch network. This information was communicated in a best practice handbook, which included:

- suggestions for how to deal with customers;
- procedures for progressing applications;
- ways to identify leads and respond to sales opportunities.

As we developed our best practice experience, we refined our communication materials, developing the 'Toolbox' – a notebook that includes sample documents and other materials to help branch staff with the practical implementation of the best practice guidelines.

It is important to note that in our best practice reviews, branch staff were intrinsically involved in the analysis and development of guidelines. This staff involvement was vital for the acceptance and viability of the project's recommendations and so for the success of the project as a whole.

Also vital for the success of the project was the use of measurement methodologies, enabling us to identify the potential for improvement, to set targets, and to track progress. Benchmarking and activity-based costing will continue to prove valuable in this ongoing improvement.

Procurement

Each year, Abbey National spends considerable sums of money – about half a billion pounds – to acquire a wide range of items including consumables, furniture, vehicles, services, buildings and computers. Despite this, we found in the early 1990s that although the company had a group purchasing department, it was responsible for less than 20 per cent of annual expenditure. Furthermore, there was no overall company strategy with regard to procurement.

Given Abbey National's constant strategic goal of enhancing company efficiency, this seemed an area ripe for improvement. It was clear, moreover, that the purchasing department possessed specialist skills that could benefit the entire company.

Objectives of the review

A company-wide procurement review was initiated, the overall aim of which was to examine procurement practices and propose ways to improve the professionalism, effectiveness and cost efficiency of our purchasing activities. Specifically, the objectives were:

- to document existing procurement practices;
- to establish future purchasing requirements i.e. effective demand management;
- to propose a procurement strategy;
- to identify cost reduction opportunities;
- to document good practices;
- to determine goals for staff training;
- to propose an implementation plan taking risks into consideration.

In short, we had to ensure a fully integrated approach to procurement encompassing people, processes and technology.

Process

In keeping with best practice, the initial phase of the review was a fact-finding activity aimed at answering the following questions:

- What is purchased by the various departments?
- How is negotiation conducted and how is the success of the procurement evaluated?
- What quantities and values are involved?
- What policies, procedures, controls and practices are adopted?
- What is the cost of purchasing operations?
- Who are the main suppliers and how are they chosen?
- What training have negotiators had?
- How is the effectiveness of purchasing measured?
- What are future procurement requirements?

The second phase concentrated on analysing the information obtained with particular emphasis on identifying cost reduction drivers and opportunities for a more strategic approach to procurement.

The next phase involved the drafting of proposals, discussions with key managers, and the preparation of final recommendations to executive directors.

In the end, the report recognized that company-wide organizational changes were necessary to ensure:

- the development of skilled staff;
- the maintenance of specialist knowledge in key procurement areas;
- the provision of a professional support service to departments where procurement is a part-time but important component of an individual's role;
- the monitoring and evaluation of the performance of all procurement activity.

Outcomes

Though stopping well short of completely altering the way Abbey National purchases goods and services, the review yielded valuable changes, including defining and centralizing the strategy for procurement and adjusting responsibilities for carrying out purchasing activities. We undertook a rationalization of suppliers in key areas such as travel, company cars, and storage; and we renegotiated major print contracts.

We set ourselves the challenging target of achieving savings of about £15 million in the first year, and we achieved that. The IT procurement team alone saved £6 million in the first year. But these early results are immediate savings only, and we will continue to see benefits from the review because of the establishment of improved procedures.

The review set forth strategies and policies, including best practice guidelines, which were published in a new Group Procurement Policy Handbook and a code of conduct for procurement staff. The publication, distributed to all employees who were responsible for purchasing, represented the first time a company-wide policy for procurement had been communicated. In addition, the company's legal department developed a policy for procurement contracts.

Our specialist procurement staff provide consulting services for the entire Group. The review did not propose that all purchasing duties be performed by the Procurement Department. Rather, it proposed that staff currently performing purchasing duties in other areas of the company continue to perform those duties and receive training to help them do that as effectively as possible. When needed, the Procurement Department remains a resource for information and advice. So more important than the immediate savings resulting from the procurement review are the procedures and policies set in place that will help create value for the Group over the long term.

Procurement represents significant expenditure within Abbey National – sufficiently large that specific challenges are being set as part of the Group planning and strategy process. We will continue to work with suppliers to reduce costs and make the company more efficient and we will work internally to instill the ethos of increasing value for money.

Service quality

At the time of writing in 1997, Abbey National's vision is 'To be the outstanding financial services company in the UK'. The statement accurately reflects our current desire not necessarily to be the biggest, but to be the best.

Competition in the industry has led – appropriately so – to a greater emphasis on the customer. Indeed, the success of Abbey National is to a large degree dependent on its ability to acquire and retain customers, and this is best accomplished through delivering a high quality of service.

Abbey National had developed and maintained a popular image as a customer-friendly institution (owing no doubt in part to our traditional building society values). A Quality Service Group chaired by the Group's Chief Executive was already in place; but there was no formal strategy for delivering quality service.

Abbey National's focus on the customer was to be the core of our quality strategy. In fact, the company's service quality review, which sought to establish company-wide policies on delivering excellent service, grew out of a project of much smaller scope, an evaluation of the way we handled customer complaints.

The creation of Abbey National's service quality strategy was aided by the company's decision to sponsor a position at the Manchester Business School. The position, which was filled by Professor John Murphy, was that of Professor of Service Quality, the first such position created in the UK. A condition of Abbey National's sponsoring this position allowed the professor to provide consulting services to the company, and this yielded the review of Abbey National's approach to quality.

Service quality review

The service quality review conducted in 1995 sought to identify needs and possible solutions for ensuring that Abbey National maintains high standards with respect to the way we serve our customers. More specifically, the objectives of the review were:

- to examine current practices that affect service quality in Abbey National;
- to identify strengths and areas for improvement;
- to make recommendations for the formalization of a service strategy that would contribute towards the goal of being the outstanding financial services company in the UK.

The service quality review began with a thorough investigation into the attitudes, practices, and opinions of a cross-section of Abbey National staff. A review team conducted semi-structured interviews with various selected managerial and front-line personnel, and self-completion questionnaires were completed by more than 150 employees who interact daily with customers.

The review also gathered information from existing sources. Abbey National already had in place a series of Employee Opinion Surveys and a customer feedback and research programme, known as RRATE, which solicited customers' opinions on our reliability, responsiveness, assurance, tangibles and empathy.

Drawing from this information, Professor Murphy produced a

report that outlined numerous prerequisites for the improvement of service quality:

- leadership and commitment from senior management;
- recruitment training and development policies;
- service quality standards and specifications;
- effective two-way communications;
- employee empowerment policies.

Employee input

The drive to achieve service quality excellence represented a significant challenge, against which we have made significant progress. The formalization of the 'Service Commitment' was the first critical step in unifying the work force around a common objective. A competition in the staff newsletter asked people to submit their suggestions for a statement that would summarize Abbey National's commitment to service quality, and using language from the entries we formed this statement:

> **Abbey National is committed to being reliable, responsive and efficient in order to retain the confidence and loyalty of its customers – delivering service you can trust.**

Strategy

Having gained the input of employees in identifying and articulating the direction of the change, we were able to establish more specific approaches to improving the quality of Abbey National's customer service.

We formulated a service quality strategy, built around the following six elements:

- customer focus – increasing customer loyalty;
- quality systems/processes – developing cost effective procedures;
- employee involvement – promoting the 'people' factor and empowering staff to provide outstanding service;
- training – ensuring that employees are equipped to meet present and future business needs;
- measurement – developing reliable means for measuring quality;

● continuous improvement – undertaking corrective action and creating new procedures, services, and products.

The integration process is to be facilitated by effective internal and external communications.

For each of these elements, we formulated action plans, which were in the early stages of implementation when this article was written, but the indications are positive that they will continue to guide us towards our goals. We recognize that for the plans to be successful, as with any other successful quality service initiative, communication is vital. We need to keep staff posted on what we're doing and continually solicit their ideas and opinions.

Conclusion

Abbey National's experience in managing these projects has confirmed that certain principles lie behind most successful efforts to manage change. In most cases, we benefited from:

● taking a systematic approach;

● ensuring ownership of the project at all levels, from executive directors down;

● minimizing the use of external consultants;

● providing for the transfer of skills to Abbey National staff when we *did* use external consultants; and

● communicating findings/proposals effectively to staff.

Experience has also revealed the benefits of using the Balanced Business Scorecard, a tool that allows managers to see the big picture and to assess both the need for change and the progress of projects aimed at producing change. Such a flexible tool allows for the co-ordination of numerous business activities. It allows for the oversight of the entire change cycle:

● measurement of current performance;

● review of practices;

● implementation of strategies;

● assessment of success.

Throughout this change cycle, we place significant importance on the development of measurement techniques such as benchmarking and activity-based costing. Through these techniques, we begin the change process by gathering information about current performance and identifying areas for improvement. The information then feeds into the strategy and planning process, and we assess our progress by using the same measurement techniques that identified the opportunities in the first place.

In the future, we will continue to place an emphasis on using benchmarking to identify opportunities for improvement. Activity-based costing, as well, will give us accurate measures of our efficiency and will show us where to devote resources.

Although our tools for measuring our position will remain the same, our frame of reference will grow. We will place increasing emphasis on international and non-financial forums which will give us greater access to benchmarking and best practice information from major European and multinational companies.

At the end of the day, effective change is required. We will continue to link performance with rewards and ensure that we are able to monitor progress. When change does happen, it should be absolutely transparent to all. The change should result in measurable improvements that customers, employees and shareholders can see and feel.

Bibliography

Armstrong, K. (1995) 'As easy as ABC: Activity Based Costing', *Administrator*, July.

Gilbert, J. (1992) *How To Eat an Elephant*, Tudor.

Kaplan, R. S. and Norton, D. P. (1993) 'Putting the Balanced Scorecard to Work', *Harvard Business Review*, September–October, pp. 134–147.

McTaggart, J. M., Kontes, P. W. and Mankins, M. C. (1994) *The Value Imperative*, Free Press.

Professor John Murphy (1993) *Service Quality and Practice*, Gill & MacMillen.

Newing, R. (1995) 'Wake up to the balanced scorecard', *Management Accounting*, March.

Oakland, J. S. (1995) *Total Quality Management*, Butterworth-Heinemann.

CHAPTER THREE

Building stronger customer relationships through the customer service chain

Ken Littlewood, formerly Head,
of Network Development,
Midland Bank

The importance of customer loyalty

During the 1990s the competitive pressures in the financial services industry have increased significantly. In the UK market this has occurred first through the growth of traditional competitors, such as the Lloyds Bank take-over of the Cheltenham and Gloucester Building Society and subsequent merger with the TSB; the merger of Halifax and Leeds building societies; and the trend for building societies and insurance companies to move into a wider range of personal financial services products. It has also occurred through new companies entering the market. For example, Richard Branson's Virgin Group is now a significant player in the PEP market and is increasing its range of products; Marks and Spencer is now a major provider of financial services; and many organizations are seeing advantages in providing plastic-based payment facilities to their customers – *The Sunday Times* and the Ford Motor Company, amongst many others, now operate Visa cards.

The danger for an organization such as the Midland Bank is that, increasingly, the most profitable parts of the service proposition for personal customers could be taken by other providers. Many of the new entrants into financial services can make considerable savings, particularly on delivery costs, giving them a pricing advantage. Furthermore, sustainable competitive advantage cannot be achieved by the high street banks through product differentiation. Advances in current systems capabilities would in most cases allow competitors to match them almost overnight.

The key competitive advantage which the banks and building societies have, however, is their existing customer base and the quality of their relationship with it. If these customers can be served satisfactorily, they are likely to remain loyal to the bank and to purchase an increasing number of services.

Research by Reicheld and Sasser (1990) has shown that customer retention is a key factor in most service companies' profitability. They have estimated that companies can boost their profits by as much as 100 per cent by retaining just 5 per cent more of their customers. They also conclude that the financial services industry's profits are particularly sensitive to achieving high customer retention rates.

Nearly three-quarters of the identifiable reasons why customers switch to an alternative bank are related to the quality of service. Hence, if financial service providers can achieve high customer satisfaction levels, then customer retention and a growth in customer relationships will result. It is clear that the future profitability of a bank's retail customer base depends on achieving low customer defection rates.

The customer service chain

Research by Heskett and his colleagues (1994) has developed the concept of the 'service profit chain'. In essence, this states that 'internal service quality' (or the quality of service support to front-line staff) is the driver of employee satisfaction, which in turn is a key driver to 'external service quality' (or good customer service) and hence customer satisfaction. Customer satisfaction then drives customer retention and hence profits. In this way all the elements of the service chain are integral to the achievement of customer retention and profitability.

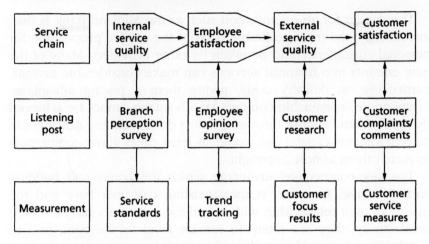

Fig. 3.1 Listening posts and measurements along the customer service chain.

The key elements of this service chain have been taken by Mildland and other banks and used as a basis for developing and co-ordinating service quality initiatives across the organization. These are shown diagrammatically in Figure 3.1.

The key to success in the management of the customer service chain is to establish a series of 'listening posts' at each stage to provide a clear understanding of the concerns and issues that arise. These, in turn, can be used to determine suitable measures of performance that allow a progress tracking system to be established. Experience gained in the management of each element of this service chain is described below.

Customer satisfaction

The starting point for the management of the service chain is to have in place a range of opportunities to listen to what customers are saying and to understand their requirements. This need not be undertaken as an expensive research project. For example, it is estimated that, on a typical day, Midland Bank has contact with around a million of its customers in various ways. Understanding what issues are driving customers' concerns, and capturing this in a meaningful way, provides an important source of information.

A regular source of interaction is customer complaints. However, experience suggests that this can give a distorted view of the day-today concerns of customers. Although this information should not be ignored, it should complement other sources. Midland Bank has found that there is no substitute for establishing processes that can track the issues that customers raise in their branch visits and their telephone calls.

Midland has set up a system in a number of branches, as well as the central Customer Service Centre, whereby staff record comments and observations made by customers, both the good and the bad. Many of these can be dealt with locally and can form a useful agenda within a branch or call centre for continuous improvement. Those that cannot be dealt with locally are escalated upwards, and priorities can be identified and tracked. The key to the success of this process is having a good way of categorizing comments and issues, so that they can be analysed easily.

In addition, local meetings and focus groups with customers are encouraged so that an agenda for improvement can be established. Midland has found that the issues that are raised through these initiatives are particularly important at times of significant change, and where the re-engineering of processes is altering the way in which customer interfaces are handled. This has been a vital source of information, for example, as back office processes have been removed from the branch network to central operations centres.

In addition to the need to listen to issues of concern to customers, it is also important to have well focused customer service measures within the management information reporting system, and that these are given suitable priority. Midland has developed a number of simple measures of service quality that can be measured at branch, area, division and national levels as a focal point for measuring customer satisfaction. These are as follows:

- *Acquisition* – this is the rate by which a business unit can attract new personal and business customers. A major reason for customers choosing a bank is through personal recommendation, so good service can drive up acquisition rates.

- *Retention* – this is the rate at which a business unit is losing customers. It is particularly easy for financial institutions to track this because a customer needs to take some positive action to close his relationship. This is a critical measure of service performance at all levels of the organization.

- *Head office complaints* – this is a measure of the number of complaints received at head office, typically normalized per 1,000 customers. Whereas complaints at a local level should in many ways be encouraged, because this allows problems to be corrected, complaints at head office indicate that the local relationship has broken down. A low level of complaints, particularly those associated with staff attitude, is a useful measure of service quality.

● *Cross sell* – this measures the depth of customer relationships. It tracks the total number of products held by a business unit, per customer. This is a good measure of how confident customers feel about their banking relationships, as the greater the level of confidence, the more products are likely to be purchased.

● *Customer focus index* – through various customer surveys and mystery shopping exercises indices of performance can be established (see external service quality section below).

By tracking these measures, relative performance and best practice can be established between business units. They also provide the basis for establishing a reward mechanism for good performance.

In 1996 Midland introduced a recognition award based on these measures. All staff in a branch that manages to improve performance from one quarter to another on all the measures receive a customer service award. This helps the measures to have a high profile at business unit level, and progress to be reviewed on a quarterly basis.

External service quality

Midland has also taken a more structured approach to identifying the main drivers of customer satisfaction. Through regular market research exercises, Midland has identified those key attributes of good service quality that customers consider important, and established relative weightings for these. These are reviewed continuously, so the list is refreshed and updated, in the light of progress made and changing customer priorities.

These attributes are used as the basis for development and monitoring of the customer focus index referred to above. This is achieved in various ways. A national postal survey regularly samples a small number of customers and tracks the bank's overall performance on each of the attributes. Some of these attributes are concerned with bank policy, others with local branch performance.

To track individual branches, a major survey of customers is conducted regularly. This has sometimes been achieved through a random sample questionnaire, and sometimes as a survey of customers who have carried out a specific transaction (e.g. opened an account or taken out a loan). This allows branches to receive direct feedback on their perceived performance at a local level. In addition, this measure is supplemented by mystery shopper visits to record performance and also to provide feedback to the branch for performance improvement and to facilitate a learning process. These results are aggregated into a single customer focus index measurement which links into the service quality measures identified above.

Employee satisfaction

Another element of a good service quality management process is a system that can regularly identify issues of major concern to employees. Without identifying these and taking the necessary steps to correct them, it is difficult for an organization to maintain sufficient levels of employee motivation.

This can be tracked as part of the ongoing personal development/review and internal communications process. However, some banks and financial institutions achieve this through a detailed employee satisfaction survey. This has the advantage of determining a few key priorities for action, and by carrying out the exercise regularly, it is possible to identify trends and to track performance. Over the last year, for example, the Hong Kong Bank of Canada has extended its incentive plans, streamlined paperwork and improved its appraisal process based on feedback from employee surveys.

It is particularly useful in this area to establish relative standards through benchmarking. This allows performance on particular employee attitude measures to be judged in relative rather than absolute terms against, for example, other companies in the UK, other financial institutions or companies undergoing a significant change.

Internal service quality

The measurement of internal service quality parallels results gained from customers in terms of what is important to them and how service can be improved. It is essential to have a regular measurement of the performance and levels of service that are provided to branches and front-line staff by support departments. This reinforces the need for every part of the organization to be involved in the customer service chain.

Each month Midland samples fifty branches and these are required to rate the quality of service provided by a number of head office departments and support functions. These support activities include IT Help Desks, Customer Service Centres, District Service Centres, Mortgage Processing Centres, Self-Service Support and Distribution Services. Branches are asked to mark the quality of service received on a range of attributes and to identify any particular problems that they find require attention.

The support functions involved are required to contact branches that give any scores below accepted target levels or raise issues of particular concern. This has been found to be a useful exercise in opening up communications between support departments and branches. The process allows each department to develop a clearer understanding of where to focus attention to meet customer's and front-line employees' needs.

Again, Midland has found this exercise to be particularly useful at times of significant change as it allows a fast response to issues of concern to be implemented quickly.

Based on this branch perception survey, a range of service-level agreements have been established between support functions and front-line staff. This again forms the basis for providing measurable service support criteria against which performance can be tracked. These would cover such areas as error rates and response times.

Conclusion – integrating the service chain

The concept of the service chain has proved to be very useful in integrating all activities concerned with service quality management. Managing the whole customer service chain, and establishing listening opportunities and measurements along it, provides an important and focused framework for improving customer service. Ultimately the whole process is directed towards improving customer satisfaction and hence customer retention.

In isolation, however, the service chain is not sufficient. To be successful customer service needs to be at the heart of an organization's culture and operations. The lead needs to be given and reinforced from the top, and supported through internal communications and training programmes.

Since 1994 Midland's customer retention levels have improved, market share has increased and customer satisfaction measures have been on an upward trend. The profile of customer service has improved throughout the organization.

Financial institutions are recognizing the need to shift the competitive focus from products to people. Increasingly it is apparent that product differentiation can be duplicated by others relatively quickly. However, the quality and history of a bank's relationship with its customers does provide a real basis for competitive advantage. Future success relies on getting this right, as this is the one aspect of a banking service which cannot be copied by the competition.

March 1997

References

Heskett, J. L. Ltd. (1994) 'Putting the Service Profit Chain to Work', *Harvard Business Review*, March–April.

Reicheld, F. and Sasser, W. (1990) 'Zero Defections: Quality Comes to Services', *Harvard Business Review*, September–October.

CHAPTER FOUR

Using the business excellence model to drive change

Leslie Ross, formerly Director of Business Systems, Mortgage Express

Introduction

Managing the ever-increasing rate of strategic change has become the critical business challenge of the '90s. Jack Welch CEO of GEC said: 'When the rate of change inside an organization is less than the external rate of change in its environment then that organization is very likely to fail to maintain its competitive position and fail.' The need for change in the financial services sector is driven by a combination of factors. The industry has over-capacity; it is often criticized for delivering poor service quality, and the combination of advances in technology, deregulation and the emergence of new competitors such as Tesco, Ford and Virgin have created major external pressures for change. However, deeply embedded cultural problems throughout the industry present serious barriers to change. Yet when one looks at other sectors, we find some remarkable examples of successful corporate turnarounds. Looking at Total Quality Award winners, it is evident that companies like Rank Xerox, Rover Group and ICL have all stared into the abyss but managed to turn themselves around, to become recognized as centres of business excellence.

The Mortgage Express turnaround

The process of stepping back from the brink and delivering a remarkable turnaround is also true in the brief story of Mortgage Express. The strategic change was forced upon us by the changing dynamics of the UK housing market which went from the boom of the Thatcher era in the 1980s to the bust of the 1990s. Other companies have found themselves in similar positions, but Mortgage Express is possibly unique in the way that the management team approached the problems forced upon them. The company's recovery has been due to the development of an approach which balances the needs of customers, employees and shareholders. The cornerstones of this approach have been:

- a fundamental belief in the capability of our people;
- widespread application of Total Quality concepts;
- A willingness to challenge every aspect of our operations; and
- A major and developing programme of two-way communications.

A commitment to excellence

This case study will show how we used the Business Excellence Model from the European Foundation for Total Quality and the British Quality Foundation to shape and develop the transformation process (Figure 4.1). It will also explain the value achieved from using this 'balanced scorecard' to actually help identify opportunities for improvement. Finally it will describe our experiences in using it to focus effort on the key 'enablers' and interest groups in the organization.

The model provides a framework against which companies can assess their performance. The percentages show the relative weightings of each element in assessing an organization's overall performance. The company has adopted the Business Excellence Model into its planning and development cycle. The model is used in 'Quality fitness reviews' to identify improvement opportunities and to build them into business plans. These facilitated workshops are usually carried out at board and management team level and everyone in the organization is given an opportunity to contribute.

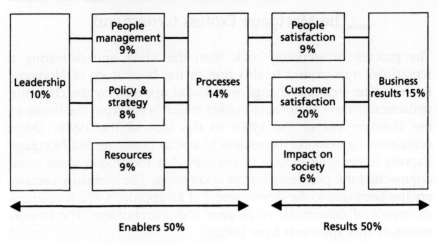

Fig. 4.1 The business excellence model.

We believe this is a great success story. The turnaround in the financial results has been dramatic. Our results on the other key drivers of employee and customer satisfaction are also remarkable. There have been a number of significant external acknowledgements of our achievements on the road to transformation. Mortgage Express achieved recognition as Investors in People in 1993 and was then shortlisted by the British Quality Foundation for the 1995 UK Quality Award. In 1996 Mortgage Express was recognized by the Crosby Foundation and received a Beacons of Quality Award, one of only forty-two companies to receive this award world-wide over the last ten years. A major accolade was then achieved when winning the 1996 UK Quality Award jointly with Ulster Carpet Mills.

Alongside these major formal external assessments of our performance, we have a range of mechanisms in place to ensure continuous feedback on our performance against the needs and expectations of each of our stakeholder group. Mortgage Express today has at the heart of its values the principle that the interests of the customers, shareholders and employees are all equal, and that it is only through balancing these that sustainable economic results can be achieved. Hence the interests of each of these stakeholder groups must be taken into account when managing change. The outcomes are reflected in long-term growth in share-holder value, the retention of loyal customers and a happy and developing workforce.

Background to Mortgage Express

Mortgage Express was formed in 1986 as a subsidiary of TSB Bank plc. It is one of the centralized mortgage lenders. These differ from the traditional mortgage lenders – banks and building societies – because they don't have branch networks, but raise finance through the money market. The primary objective in establishing such a business is to create a low-cost centralized operation which can provide a fast and more convenient service.

The late 80s saw activity in the housing market reach new heights and property prices soared. Mortgage Express was one of the fastest-growing lenders. Between 1986 and 1990 our mortgage assets increased to over £3 billion, with over 50,000 customers. However, the situation changed rapidly in the early 90s, and the housing market's dramatic expansion turned and collapsed. Mortgage Express was hit hard by the collapse and by late 1990 was losing money because of increasing bad debts. In 1991, TSB took a strategic decision that Mortgage Express would stop taking new mortgages and would withdraw from the market over the following two or three years.

By April 1991 TSB appointed a new management team at Mortgage Express with the objective of restoring financial stability to minimize potential loss. At this point the transformation process and the quest for Total Quality began.

The road to quality

The first task was to identify and tackle our key problems. The need to get things right and to stabilize the situation meant that we had to undertake a truly fundamental review to surface and address the root causes of the huge issues facing the company. The sales and marketing department were all but closed down, with only a small team remaining to handle customer communication and retention activity. Employees were redeployed into arrears management and related activities. We re-engineered our processes, upgraded our technology infrastructure, overhauled our financial management systems and improved the quality of management information. The motivation of our people was critical to our success, but trust in management was at rock bottom. This was not surprising, as the assumption was that the business would close – everyone expected to lose their job within two to three years! In late 1991, we commissioned MORI to carry out employee opinion research and introduced a strategy to tackle the problems identified.

There were many key areas to be addressed on the road to profitability. The first phase of the problem was dealt with by creating a new control-oriented environment. The business was in effect run as a 'master project', with key initiatives run as sub-projects. Each of the management team had specific objectives and targets which had to be met if the overall change programme was to be delivered. By 1992 the business had been brought under control and the team were meeting their targets. We recognized that the next stage of the transformation required us to move from an environment which focused on controls towards a culture which emphasized Total Quality and encouraged ownership and participation. Hence it was decided to initiate a Total Quality programme and start training everyone in Total Quality tools and techniques. In 1992 the first 'Quality fitness review' using the Business Excellence model was completed. As a result we upgraded our approach to continuous service improvement based on customer feedback.

The 1993 Fitness review identified the need for a unifying vision. Everyone was involved in redefining the mission and values, and pursuit of Total Quality became our unifying and driving force. The new mission is called 'The Way Ahead':

Our aim is to be recognized as a top quality company. Working together as a team we shall achieve this by:

- providing our customers with a first class service;
- maximizing long-term value for our shareholder (TSB);
- enabling our employees to achieve their best.

Working together means living our values:

Teamwork: Everybody matters and has a valid point of view.

Integrity: We are open, honest and fair in everything we do.

Recognition: We praise achievement and celebrate success.

Quality: We deliver what we promise and constantly seek to improve.

Today almost every company has a mission statement, but in many cases these are treated with cynicism and contempt by management and staff alike. The difference at Mortgage Express is that we mean it and strive to live it. For us, the launch of 'The Way Ahead' was not an end in itself, but was used instead as the driver for our organizational and culture change.

Our staff opinion research in 1996 showed that 90 per cent of the staff believe in the mission and values. Encouragingly, 80 per cent of them thought that their boss did too!

The Balanced Scorecard

One aspect of Mortgage Express's success has been its ability to maintain a sense of balance. The European/UK Quality model (Figure 4.1) fits the culture because its nine sections encourage managers to focus on a range of activity within a company. Employees can relate to it and it fits into the planning cycle, ensuring that there are clear links between leadership, policy and strategy (formulation and communication), people management, resource planning and processes. A balanced business is seen as one where all the elements are working together to achieve the right results.

Mortgage Express has used the model as a key component of its strategic planning and operational planning processes. This includes planning and prioritization of the Total Quality programme. Below are provided a few examples of what has been achieved through addressing each of the key 'enablers'.

Leadership

Mortgage Express has a strong emphasis on face-to-face communications as a means of building trust and ensuring that messages are delivered and understood consistently. There is now a well-developed employee communication process. (See Figure 4.2.)

There is a clear team-briefing process which cascades information from top to bottom of the organization, and Total Quality is a key item in these briefings. There is also a well-established practice of special events to involve people in change through director-led sessions on quality and operational change. The communications effort is high and there is an acceptance that you cannot communicate enough about change, mission and vision. For example, between 1991 and 1996 we conducted over 350 director-led briefings, held more than 1,800 team briefings and ran twenty 'fun events' for the whole company.

At the launch of 'The Way Ahead' programme Keith Greenough, Chief Executive, attended meetings with all employees, in small

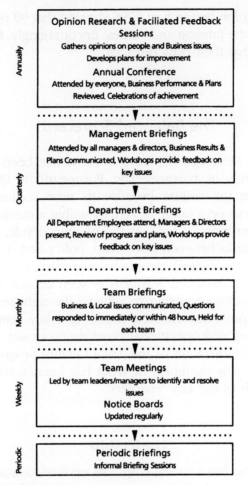

Fig. 4.2 Employee communication process.

groups, engaging in open two-way discussions on the impact that this change would have on the business.

A key part of leadership is listening to staff. Each department has a quarterly meeting. Keith has attended over 100 of these and other directors often sit in on meetings other than their own. All directors and managers also hold more regular meetings where people can air views in an open and honest way. It is important to keep these spontaneous and innovative. By 1994 a sharp increase in people's satisfaction with communications had been achieved, showing effectiveness in these changes.

In order to demonstrate top-down commitment when undertaking Total Quality training, all directors and managers received training

Fig. 4.3 Leadership review cycle.

alongside more junior employees. In 1993 a culture change programme was launched. Directors, managers and team leaders all participated in open discussion groups. The Director of Human Resources and Quality, Peter Taylor, ran a major part of the programme. As part of the process of developing leadership skills at all levels of the organization, over one-third of the workforce went through training in facilitation and problem-solving skills.

Another key element is the recognition of individuals and teams. These have to be refreshed constantly to stimulate interest and participation. Directors and managers play a central role in recognition events and ceremonies.

The leadership challenge is accepted by managers in the organization as a personal development requirement. An annual review cycle which includes a 360-degree appraisal system based on best practice is accepted by all directors and managers, and results are displayed openly (see Figures 4.3 and 4.4).

Policy and strategy

The mission 'to be recognised as a Top Quality Company' is the bedrock on which we build our policies and strategies. Implementation is driven through the strategic planning process. This has to be responsive to the need for change at any time. The opportunity for feedback from customers, staff and suppliers is built into the process to ensure their involvement and participation. Every employee must understand our policies and strategies to perform their job satisfac-

- Inspire a shared vision
  - Envision the future
  - Enlist others
- Challenge the Process
  - Search for opportunities
  - Experiment and take risks
- Enable others to act
  - Foster collaboration
  - Strengthen others
- Model the Process
  - Set the example
  - Plan small wins
- Encourage the Heart
  - Recognize individuals and teams
  - Celebrate achievements

Fig. 4.4 Leadership best practice.

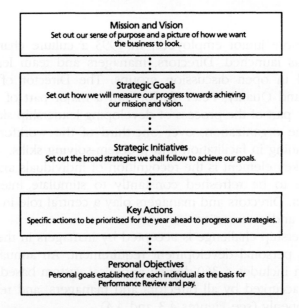

Mission and Vision
Set out our sense of purpose and a picture of how we want the business to look.

Strategic Goals
Set out how we will measure our progress towards achieving our mission and vision.

Strategic Initiatives
Set out the broad strategies we shall follow to achieve our goals.

Key Actions
Specific actions to be prioritised for the year ahead to progress our strategies.

Personal Objectives
Personal goals established for each individual as the basis for Performance Review and pay.

Fig. 4.5 Deployment process.

torily. A high priority is placed on this with an annual presentation to all staff, followed by detailed departmental briefings and quarterly updates on progress and future plans (see Figure 4.5).

The strategic planning process was benchmarked and as a result improvements were introduced. A key element of this is data-gathering. There is an annual cycle which starts with research into the economic environment. This is followed by a series of workshops where the board develops its thinking and views and identifies

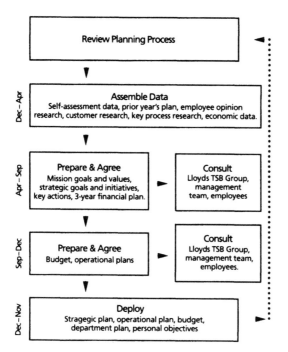

Fig. 4.6 Annual planning cycle.

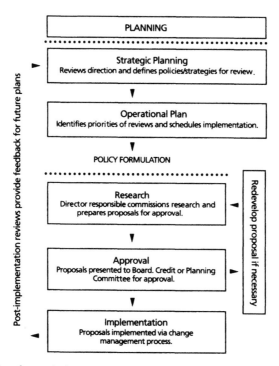

Fig. 4.7 Policy formulation process.

the relevant political threats, social changes and technical developments. An analysis of strengths, weaknesses, opportunities and threats (SWOT) is also undertaken (see Figures 4.6 and 4.7).

To these are added the feedback from the Quality fitness review, customer and staff opinion surveys. The strategic objectives and key actions are then developed into a three-year plan. Key actions for year one are expanded to prepare the annual operational plan and budget. These are reviewed and then communicated through the management structure to all employees.

Outside the formal planning cycle, the Board reviews and changes policy whenever necessary. Such matters are considered each month at our board-level committees. Feedback on business results, customer and employee satisfaction is examined monthly. Deviations from expected results are investigated and where necessary additional reviews of polices and strategies are scheduled. Employees are encouraged to raise policy issues with managers and directors as and when they arise.

People management

In 1991, after the business withdrawal announcement, employee morale was at rock bottom. Everyone was threatened with redundancy within two to three years. It was identified quickly that there was a need to put people on the strategic agenda. A human resource strategy was developed and delivered.

Our goal of enabling people to achieve their best is an integral part of the mission. Strategic objectives and key actions to achieve this goal are built into our plans. A great amount of effort is taken to ensure initiatives are both interesting and fun.

As already stated, our employee opinion questionnaire is the cornerstone of our continuous improvement in people management. We began surveys in 1991. For two years we employed MORI to conduct individual interviews and group discussions, and around 15 per cent of employees participated. Following the 1993 Quality fitness review, an in-house team was formed to review the employee feedback process. Involving people has been a feature ever since, and has been instrumental in tackling real areas of concern. The annual staff opinion survey provides quantitative information which is communicated openly to all employees who come back with suggestions on improvement opportunities. We develop action plans based on this feedback.

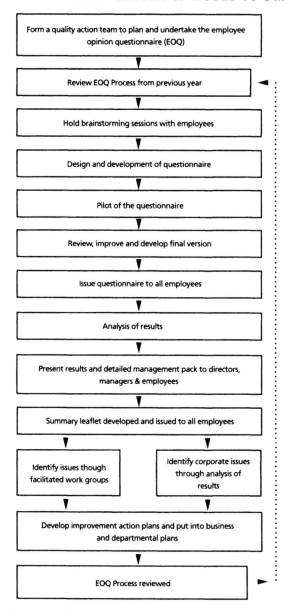

Fig. 4.8 Employee opinion questionnaire.

The process itself was reviewed again in 1994. A team of volunteers formed a Quality Action Team (QAT). The new process is outlined in Figure 4.8.

The human resources strategy placed an emphasis on continuous and substantial improvement in:

- Aligning objectives with corporate goals.

- Management style and leadership.

- An appraisal system that focuses on performance review and development opportunities.

- Effective top-down and bottom-up communication – we introduced and publish a communications policy which covers regular and periodic communications, and we constantly review the effectiveness of our communications.

- Terms and conditions of employment.

- Training and development – a culture that promotes continuous employee development through both internal and external courses and further education.

- Computer-based training – a cost-effective means of developing a flexible training base.

- Open learning – maintaining a centre where employees can access job related and personal development resources including videos, books and audio tapes. This is supported enthusiastically and promoted through innovative techniques, such as an 'open learning trolley' that visits all departments once a month.

- Teamwork – an ethic which is a very strong part of our culture. We train our staff in project management and facilitation skills.

- Promotion of involvement and empowerment through involving individuals and teams in quality improvement.

- Customer and supplier meetings – to resolve interface issues involving customer-facing staff.

- A quality recognition scheme which rewards quality behaviour and achievement and encourages praise for a job well done.

- Ceremonies and activities – focused on our principle that work should be fun, and embodied in our value: 'We praise achievement and celebrate success'.

In 1994 our culture change programme showed that people had a perception that the culture was heavily power- and role-orientated – probably not a surprising outcome when considering the heavily directed phase in 1991/2. By 1995 there was a move in perception to more of a task and people culture, reflecting our effort to achieve greater levels of empowerment and devolved responsibility (see Figures 4.9 and 4.10).

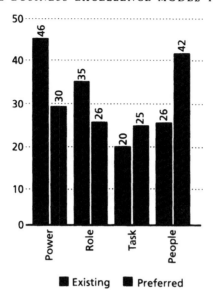

Fig. 4.9 Perceptions of cultures – 1994.

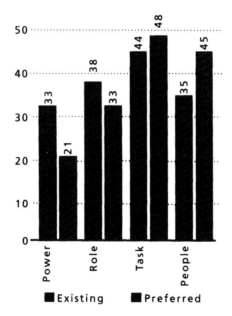

Fig. 4.10 Perceptions of cultures – 1995.

Resources

Mortgage Express works to a three-year financial plan with an associated one-year budget. A comprehensive pack of management information is produced each month and is used to monitor actual performance against expected outturn. The business has developed sophisticated processes to manage its key financial parameters with an objective to increase shareholder value substantially.

In the context of our rapidly changing environment we reviewed our strategy for working with third party suppliers. We needed to import new skills rapidly while avoiding building our fixed cost base and to protect ourselves against the loss of key people. We adopted a strategy of outsourcing key services to major suppliers, with the common aim of delivering a 'triple win' (customer, employee and shareholder).

The management and regular review of external relationships has become an important part of the development of our business. Our approach is to work with suppliers to improve processes managed for mutual benefit. Meetings are held regularly to review progress and we run joint problem solving initiatives to review progress. We establish targets through mutual agreement and actively seek partners who are committed to Total Quality.

Outsourcing has been used where appropriate to cover key risks or where core competencies are best obtained from third parties. For example, the information technology departments were outsourced to Cap Gemini, to reduce exposure to loss of key skills. The teams have enjoyed excellent relationships and are fully integrated. People take part in Quality events, training and sports and social activity. Considerable effort is made to make it one team.

Processes

On our Total Quality journey we established the need to identify key processes. A fundamental review was undertaken in 1991 and developed into a major project which took eighteen months to complete. We needed a total redirection of resources and mapped and documented all our customer processes and set up training support using CBT training.

By 1995 it was clear that we needed significant change. This was identified through our self-assessment and through the external assessment from our 1995 UK Quality Award application. We launched our Process Review and Management Project (PRAM) with the twin objectives of identifying and prioritizing our processes and upgrading our process management approach.

We undertook a review of our high-level 'end to end' processes, agreed a revised process structure and evaluated the impact of each process on the company's strategic goals. The financial impact and impact on people and customer satisfaction were ranked as high, medium or low, and where possible, external benchmarks were used. The result is a process structure and clarification of our business processes (see Figure 4.11). The PRAM project also established a mechanism for reviewing our processes each year as part of our planning process.

The methodology for carrying out process reviews has also been delivered. The Process Review teams have delivered early successes and a major redesign project was delivered in our new business area in 1997.

Our key processes are reviewed as part of our annual planning process. They are revised to reflect changes in strategy or changes to

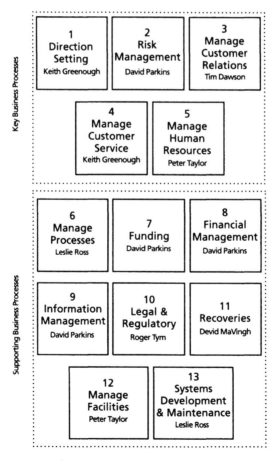

Fig. 4.11 Process overview map.

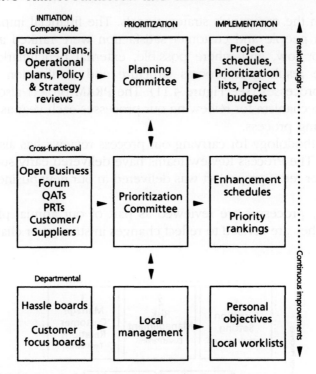

Fig. 4.12 Initiation, prioritization and implementations.

the environment. Major projects are prioritized at board level, while enhancements and changes are prioritized by managers using our Quality Improvement Process (QIP). The financial impact of our key processes is measured and our potential for performance improvement is used to guide our decisions on priorities (see Figure 4.12).

Achieving our goals demands that projects are initiated correctly and delivered against agreed requirements, on time and to specification. Hence, we have a clear initiation process (see Figure 4.13) and a well-developed project methodology (see Figure 4.14). Over 200 people have been trained in project skills since 1991.

The Total Quality Management approach encourages staff to come up with new ideas and our Change Control and QIP process enable resources to be allocated to initiatives which come from the staff. Considerable emphasis has been placed on revitalizing our approach on a regular basis to keep up interest and enthusiasm, and innovative and fun ideas are used to stimulate thinking on process improvement (see Figure 4.15).

76

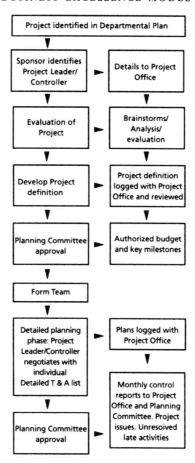

Fig. 4.13 Initiating major projects.

In defining a problem, employees at all levels often need facilitation and support. In cross-functional process issues we use a group of trained facilitators to enable the resolution of issues. Often staff need help to define possible solutions. We have created the Open Business Forum, where skilled IT staff are available daily for an hour to discuss how opportunities for improvement may be taken forward. We also use hassle boards, 'fruit trees', (where each fruit represents an idea which has provided beneficial results), 'change agent' initiatives and a Quality recognition scheme which includes 'employee of the month' and rewards for those achieving recognition.

Through our work in carrying out annual Quality fitness reviews, we have come to appreciate the linkages between the five 'enabling'

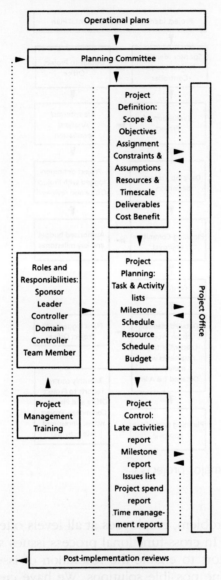

Fig. 4.14 Project management methodology.

categories of the EFQM model: leadership, policy and strategy, people management, resources, and processes. The company has demonstrated that these linkages feed directly into business results. The turnaround in Mortgage Express has been remarkable in all of the results sections: customer satisfaction, people satisfaction, impact on society, and business results.

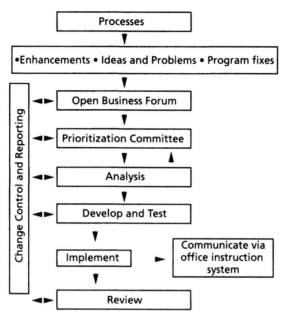

Fig. 4.15 Quality improvement process.

Customer satisfaction

Our goal is to 'provide our customers with a first-class service'. This means achieving at least 95 per cent customer satisfaction with our service delivery. This is based on an assessment of 'best in class' performance for mortgage lenders. Our strategy is to achieve this by listening to what our customers say. We record customer calls and team leaders use these to coach and develop people (see Figure 4.16).

Our key measure of overall service satisfaction with the customer service process is our customers' perception of how well their enquiry was handled. We established our baseline position with service satisfaction at around 70 per cent. Satisfaction scores continued to run at around the same level for much of 1993, but a goal of 85 per cent was achieved by October 1994. Since then, satisfaction levels have increased to new targets in the 90–95 per cent range (see Figure 4.17).

Retaining good customers has been a strategic goal since 1992. We drove customer retention rates up from virtually zero in 1992 to over 10 per cent of customers redeeming their mortgages in 1995. In an increasingly competitive mortgage market we developed a range of

Fig. 4.16 Listening to customers.

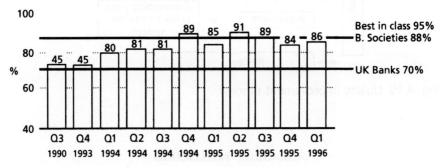

Fig. 4.17 Percent of overall service satisfaction.

new products offering long-term value for money and innovative features. The approach has been very successful and in February 1996 we retained over 40 per cent of customers redeeming their loans.

The improved financial control in Mortgage Express and the continuing trends of improvement on other key enablers encouraged a review of the strategy to close the business. In 1995 it was accepted that closure was only one of a series of options for the company and that others presented the opportunity to capitalize on the core competencies that had been developed since 1991. A pilot was launched to take Mortgage Express back into new lending and the company successfully re-entered the mortgage market as a niche player.

In 1995 we participated in a study of 'Service Britain' conducted by the London Business School. The study found that the four key drivers to superior performance were leadership, service culture,

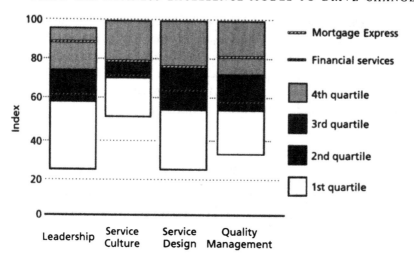

Fig. 4.18 Company feedback – positioning against service performance – UK distribution and industry average (Source: London Business School).

service design and quality management. We were benchmarked against other organizations in the study. Figure 4.18 shows our performance.

Further customer satisfaction measures have been obtained from an annual qualitative survey which is enhanced by a quantitative customer analysis. This has successfully identified key areas of customer concern and new policies have been introduced to improve performance in those areas.

People satisfaction

Our employees' perception of Mortgage Express can be measured in a number of ways. The number of staff who take the time to complete the annual opinion survey has been steadily improving since 1993, growing from 78 per cent to 85 per cent in 1996, well ahead of MORI's views of average response rate of 60 per cent. Overall satisfaction levels run at 74 per cent, well ahead of the national norm of 54 per cent (MORI).

Satisfaction with the working environment is another key measure and the management team has responded to issues raised in this section to improve the score steadily since 1993. Low scores were recorded on the office environment section, highlighting problems with the air conditioning and heating systems. These were reviewed and a firm of experts brought in to advise us as to the possible upgrade. This was duly implemented and has delivered improvements in this area. Today 77 per cent of employees are satisfied with the working environment. The emphasis on our people strategies has seen continuous and substantial improvement in all of the key areas encompassed within the HR strategy.

Impact on society

For a small company, based at a single North London site, it is difficult at first to see what could be achieved in this area. However, Mortgage Express has been both innovative and creative. The impact of the recession on many of our customers has left them in financial difficulties. We offer comprehensive support for mortgage customers in financial difficulties and have achieved an enviable reputation in the market-place. Our in-house counselling department makes over 700 personal visits per year and our service has been benchmarked by companies outside the industry. Our relationships with money advice centres and citizens' advice bureaux have been developed to provide a link to independent advice for our customers.

We participate in the Mortgage Arrears Forum (MAF) which enables lenders, counsellors, advice groups, the charity Shelter and homeless units to pass on information, exchange ideas, improve liaison and encourage business-wide best practice.

We are committed supporters of charitable causes, supporting employee initiatives and contributing to the donations. Here we are fortunate to have an association with the Lloyds/TSB Foundations which were set up on the flotation of TSB to deliver charitable support. The people in the organization have seized the opportunity to give help to worthy causes in many different areas of the community.

We are also involved in local education. We support Investors in People, host events for the North London Training and Enterprise Council and support several of their projects.

Business results

The business excellence model is based on a belief that there are strong linkages from leadership through to the other enablers, and

y used, their personal objectives and the way they were meas-
d. They also approached their customers differently, finding out
at they could afford to pay and understanding why they had
en behind with their repayments. Over a period of two years, the
ciety totally changed its debt collection processes to become one
the most effective and customer sensitive in the industry. In the
ocess it has reduced its debt provisions from 20 per cent above the
rm for the industry, to 20 per cent below.

The company

Britannia Building Society is a medium-sized company which has its
headquarters in the small industrial town of Leek in rural Staffordshire, England. At the time of writing in December 1997, its assets
are £14.9bn., it operates from 200 branches and employs 2,750
people. Its main business is providing a secure place for people's
savings which are used to finance mortgages on residential housing.
Britannia also has a number of other lines of business:

- an assurance company selling life, pensions and investment
products through independent financial advisors as well as direct
through the Building Society's branches;

- investment management, not only of policy-holders' funds but
also for third parties;

- a small network of estate agents which are becoming increasingly integrated with the Society's branches; and

- commercial lending to housing associations and small firms.

The majority of the Society's business is acquired through its
branch network, with the recently established telephone, postal and
direct sales channels now contributing between 10 and 20 per cent
of sales.

Economic background

In common with all other lenders in the sector, the economic
recession and collapse of the housing and commercial property
markets at the end of the 1980s led to a substantial increase in the

that improved business results can be achieved through a Total
Quality Management approach which pays attention to each of the
enabling elements presented in Figure 4.1 and described earlier. This
has been the case with Mortgage Express, and the financial turnaround of the company since 1992 has demonstrated the success that
can be achieved through adopting such an integrated business-wide
approach.

The transformation of profit before tax figures has been described
as remarkable by outside observers. From 1990 the business was hit
hard by the deepening recession in the housing market and underlying falls in property values and escalating arrears. Profits in the
1980s turned to losses and tremendous economic uncertainty made
predicting future performance very difficult.

In 1992, at the bottom of the economic cycle, the business made
a huge loss of £67 million. At that time we prepared a three-
year recovery plan aimed at returning to profit by 1995. With the
improving economic environment plus vastly improved effectiveness
and control, we restored the business to break-even in 1993, well
ahead of plan. The organization has since been highly profitable. In
1991–92 it lost £100m., but from 1993–96 it has made profits of
£104m.

Since 1993 the business has outperformed targets in areas within
our control. The turnaround has enabled us to achieve a higher level
of profitability than other centralized lenders of comparable size.
Shareholder value has increased greatly. Our return on capital employed is well ahead of target and is better than the average for the
top ten building societies.

The risk in the business is now greatly reduced and the business
is under financial control.

Conclusion

The accolade of winning the 1996 UK Quality Award represented
public acknowledgement for the achievement of a dream that was
put in place in 1993. From certain closure, the company has fought
its way back to profitability and is now back in the mortgage market
as a successful lender. The achievement of our aim 'to be recognized
as a top quality company' has been delivered through a deliberate
policy and clear purpose. Without leadership this could not have

been achieved but it is equally the result of the efforts of an exceptional team of people. Their professionalism, commitment and a huge sense of making it fun have been the critical ingredients in the Mortgage Express story.

Postscript During 1997 Lloyds TSB decided that the best return to shareholders would be achieved through the sale of Mortgage Express rather than through integration with the rest of their mortgage operations. The company attracted interest from ten purchasers and was sold to Bradford and Bingley Building Society in July 1997. The Team given responsibility for the business in 1991 had therefore achieved its mission.

Keith Greenough's Team now have responsibility for Bradford and Bingley's Lending business or have taken up new roles within the Society. They are thriving on the new challenge.

CHAPTER FIVE

Using business pro re-engineering to improve mortgage repayments

*Chris Lazenby, Head of Busine
Improvement, Britannia
Building Society*

Introduction

We all want to achieve radical change better in our businesses and aspire to world class servic customers. Britannia Building Society has achieved just tha unpleasant task of collecting debts from its customers in difficulty. In common with other mortgage lenders, Britannia arrears of mortgage subscriptions climb to unprecedented le the early 1990s. Determined to reduce the multi-million losses, the Society tried a new method of collecting its de *speaking* to customers who missed their monthly payments, i of writing to them.

Following a successful test of this approach, the Society duced radical changes to the way its debt collectors worked way they were organized and managed, what they had to do, individual responsibilities, skills and knowledge, the inform they received, their hours of work, the equipment and systems that improved business results can be achieved through a Total Quality Management approach which pays attention to each of the enabling elements presented in Figure 4.1 and described earlier. This has been the case with Mortgage Express, and the financial turnaround of the company since 1992 has demonstrated the success that can be achieved through adopting such an integrated business-wide approach.

The transformation of profit before tax figures has been described as remarkable by outside observers. From 1990 the business was hit hard by the deepening recession in the housing market and underlying falls in property values and escalating arrears. Profits in the 1980s turned to losses and tremendous economic uncertainty made predicting future performance very difficult.

In 1992, at the bottom of the economic cycle, the business made a huge loss of £67 million. At that time we prepared a three-year recovery plan aimed at returning to profit by 1995. With the improving economic environment plus vastly improved effectiveness and control, we restored the business to break-even in 1993, well ahead of plan. The organization has since been highly profitable. In 1991–92 it lost £100 m., but from 1993–96 it has made profits of £104 m.

Since 1993 the business has outperformed targets in areas within our control. The turnaround has enabled us to achieve a higher level of profitability than other centralized lenders of comparable size. Shareholder value has increased greatly. Our return on capital employed is well ahead of target and is better than the average for the top ten building societies.

The risk in the business is now greatly reduced and the business is under financial control.

Conclusion

The accolade of winning the 1996 UK Quality Award represented public acknowledgement for the achievement of a dream that was put in place in 1993. From certain closure, the company has fought its way back to profitability and is now back in the mortgage market as a successful lender. The achievement of our aim 'to be recognized as a top quality company' has been delivered through a deliberate policy and clear purpose. Without leadership this could not have been achieved but it is equally the result of the efforts of an exceptional team of people. Their professionalism, commitment and a huge sense of making it fun have been the critical ingredients in the Mortgage Express story.

Postscript During 1997 Lloyds TSB decided that the best return to shareholders would be achieved through the sale of Mortgage Express rather than through integration with the rest of their mortgage operations. The company attracted interest from ten purchasers and was sold to Bradford and Bingley Building Society in July 1997. The Team given responsibility for the business in 1991 had therefore achieved its mission.

Keith Greenough's Team now have responsibility for Bradford and Bingley's Lending business or have taken up new roles within the Society. They are thriving on the new challenge.

Using business process re-engineering to improve mortgage repayments

Chris Lazenby, Head of Business Improvement, Britannia Building Society

Introduction

We all want to achieve radical change for the better in our businesses and aspire to world class service for our customers. Britannia Building Society has achieved just that for the unpleasant task of collecting debts from its customers in financial difficulty. In common with other mortgage lenders, Britannia saw its arrears of mortgage subscriptions climb to unprecedented levels in the early 1990s. Determined to reduce the multi-million pound losses, the Society tried a new method of collecting its debts by *speaking* to customers who missed their monthly payments, instead of writing to them.

Following a successful test of this approach, the Society introduced radical changes to the way its debt collectors worked, the way they were organized and managed, what they had to do, their individual responsibilities, skills and knowledge, the information they received, their hours of work, the equipment and systems that they used, their personal objectives and the way they were measured. They also approached their customers differently, finding out what they could afford to pay and understanding why they had fallen behind with their repayments. Over a period of two years, the Society totally changed its debt collection processes to become one of the most effective and customer sensitive in the industry. In the process it has reduced its debt provisions from 20 per cent above the norm for the industry, to 20 per cent below.

The company

Britannia Building Society is a medium-sized company which has its headquarters in the small industrial town of Leek in rural Staffordshire, England. At the time of writing in December 1997, its assets are £14.9bn., it operates from 200 branches and employs 2,750 people. Its main business is providing a secure place for people's savings which are used to finance mortgages on residential housing. Britannia also has a number of other lines of business:

- an assurance company selling life, pensions and investment products through independent financial advisors as well as direct through the Building Society's branches;
- investment management, not only of policy-holders' funds but also for third parties;
- a small network of estate agents which are becoming increasingly integrated with the Society's branches; and
- commercial lending to housing associations and small firms.

The majority of the Society's business is acquired through its branch network, with the recently established telephone, postal and direct sales channels now contributing between 10 and 20 per cent of sales.

Economic background

In common with all other lenders in the sector, the economic recession and collapse of the housing and commercial property markets at the end of the 1980s led to a substantial increase in the number of customers having difficulty repaying their mortgages. High interest rates and falling house values placed an exceptional burden on the ability of borrowers to repay their mortgages and the numbers of customers who fell behind with their monthly subscriptions grew to unprecedented levels. Negative equity, redundancy and company failures added to the usual difficulties affecting homeowners such as marital breakdown or ill health.

In 1992, the average mortgage as a percentage of the value of the property it was financing reached record levels at 45 per cent, up from 25 per cent only four years earlier. These economic factors combined to cause significant increases in both bad debt and arrears of mortgage subscriptions. To indicate the scale of the problem, in November 1992 the Society was making the same provisions for arrears and bad debt *every working day* as they had made in the whole of 1987. This problem needed to be addressed systematically if the Society was to achieve its growth ambitions. Hence, in late 1992, Britannia launched a major project to improve control over arrears and provisioning.

Business process re-engineering at Britannia

At that time, Britannia had no formal experience of business process re-engineering. A small management services department dealt with incremental changes to the way we did business but its activities were mostly confined to 'tuning' the existing business processes within a single department. The Information Systems Department was responsible for carrying out larger technology-oriented projects but, again, these tended to be driven by the needs of a particular department in the organization, rather than by the overall needs of the entire business. There was no focal point for major cross-functional change.

Arrears collection

In 1992, arrears collection at Britannia was a laborious paper-based system, the main contact with the Society being initiated by the customer. There was little understanding of the reasons for arrears on a particular account. Our arrears collectors were measured on the number of items of post which they dealt with and the size of their backlog of cases. The Society had no effective policy or practices to differentiate between the types of arrears: we did not know if the customer had genuine hardship and could not pay, or whether they simply would not pay because of other financial pressures.

Strategy

An underlying principle was established: collecting *any* payment from borrowers in difficulty with their mortgages was better than collecting *no* payment. Customers would be helped to determine what they could afford. We knew from the published accounts of our competitors that, measured as a proportion of mortgage balances, our bad debts were significantly higher than the market. We estimated that we were making bad debt provision at a rate which was about 20 per cent higher than similar societies. As a result we decided that we would not only match the competition but that we would outperform it by that same percentage. A clear objective was set to reduce the value of arrears by 40 per cent before the end of 1994. Having set that objective, the next question was how was it to be achieved?

Getting started

The then Head of Lending undertook a survey of best practice in the industry so that we could understand how other lenders were tackling their arrears. The result of that study was a decision to change the way arrears were collected: instead of writing to our customers, we would telephone them.

This approach was tested by a team of four collectors over a short period before it was implemented throughout the Arrears Department. The early results were very encouraging. The test concentrated on borrowers who were one to two months in arrears, and achieved immediate success. Two-thirds of the agreements which our collectors made with our borrowers were honoured. Over 73 per cent of the total extra payments promised by customers were actually received by the Society.

This trial run was an essential stage before the eventual roll-out of the approach to the entire Collections Department. In particular, the initial nervousness that Britannia staff felt about talking to customers in their own homes, rather than writing to them, was quickly allayed when the customers' reaction was almost universally positive. The test became the first step in a long sequence of changes which were to take place over the following two and a half years. It affected the people involved, the technology they used, the way arrears were collected, the management reporting of arrears and the structure of the department.

Individuals and roles

The major change which affected our staff was that they had to talk to customers rather than write to them. Individual collectors were given intensive training in the techniques of negotiating agreements with customers for clearing their arrears. Telephone conversations were scripted and specialist consultants in telephone service were employed to teach staff new skills in managing calls. Collectors were empowered to negotiate agreements ranging from payment of the current mortgage subscription plus an increased amount to reduce arrears, through the payment of the current subscription so that the arrears did not grow, and even to allow the payment of a reduced subscription. Cases were allocated to individual members of staff to ensure continuity of dealings between a particular customer and collector.

In the old Arrears Department, supervisors had been senior clerks who dealt with the more difficult cases. Under the new approach, they became coaches to their team, not dealing with customers directly but instead reviewing cases with their staff, advising how they could be handled differently and keeping hour-by-hour records of the number of agreements made by individual collectors and the results achieved by their teams.

Saturday working and evening shifts were introduced to make it easier for the collectors to contact the customers at home. Staff who had previously worked nine to five were now employed from 1 pm to 9 pm. Staff spent the early afternoon reviewing their cases for that day, preparing the information they needed and deciding how to approach each customer. By early evening, the collectors were on the telephone speaking to customers and negotiating agreements for recovering the back-payments owed to the Society.

Technology

These changes were supported by a significant investment in new technology. Customers' names and addresses were sent to an external bureau to discover their telephone numbers so that they could be recorded on our systems. The Society had already pioneered the use of document image processing to scan correspondence so that it could be distributed electronically throughout the Insurance Department. Scanning was extended to the Arrears Department so that copies of all incoming and outgoing correspondence with the customer were easily accessible by every collector. Links were built between the main mortgage system and the collectors' work-stations so that, when the customer made a payment, the up-to-date financial records could be checked to see whether the payment was what had been agreed.

A 'predictive dialler' was introduced so that customers could be telephoned more efficiently. Because it was linked to the administration and correspondence systems, customers' details were automatically brought to the collectors' screens at the same time each telephone call connected. The predictive dialler alone increased the productivity of the collectors from four to twenty customer contacts per hour.

New programs were written to check the main mortgage system every day for customers whose arrears had reached a certain percentage of the outstanding balance. These cases were downloaded daily to create the 'in-tray' for each collector. Cases were automatically assigned a 'risk factor', depending on the size of the arrears in relationship to the loan, and the highest-risk cases were allocated to collectors first. As agreements for paying arrears were reached with each customer, diary entries were automatically made by the system to allow collectors to follow up and check whether the agreement was being kept. This 'account monitoring' process was further automated after the new approach had been running for some months, so that the only cases which were reallocated to collectors were those where the amounts that the customer had agreed to pay were not being received by the Society. Every contact with a customer caused the system to automatically update a 'history sheet' showing what had been agreed.

Management information and targets

Before these changes were made, the Society management had had very little insight into the nature of its arrears book. Our understanding grew progressively during the project. For example, the arrears were analysed into four categories by the percentage of the loan (less than 2.5 per cent, 2.5–5 per cent, 5–10 per cent and 10 per cent plus). This categorization caused the business to focus the allocation of collections staff onto the high-value arrears cases.

Low-value arrears (for example: where only one payment had been missed) were found to be causing a lot of 'noise', with thousands of cases moving into and out of this category every month. Many of these cases had causes within our own control. A large percentage of borrowers who missed one payment caught up without being prompted and never fell two payments behind. The collections process was changed so that, rather than a telephone call, these customers were sent letters advising them of their payment oversight. This change allowed the telephone collections teams to concentrate on cases where more than one payment had been missed.

Over time, our targeting became progressively more sophisticated, with objectives such as:

- All cases falling a second month behind should be contacted within five working days by telephone.

- Customers with good arrears repayment histories (six months or more) should be offered the opportunity to capitalize the outstanding debt.

- We would halve the number of cases going into litigation.

- We would reduce evictions by 25 per cent.

- We would collect £10m. of outstanding arrears in the first twelve months of the project. (We actually achieved £11.6m.)

- Within three months of repossessing a property, we would sell it for more than 95 per cent of its market value.

These targets served to motivate the teams in an extraordinary way. Although they had seemed out of reach when set, the majority were achieved, and some were exceeded by a wide margin.

Structure

Before the project, the responsibility for contacting customers about arrears had been shared between the Head Office and the branch. When the new approach was started, branch involvement with collections was stopped. Branch staff were asked only to obtain a customer's telephone number so that the Head Office arrears collectors could contact the customer. Although this caused some resentment amongst branch staff, it made control of arrears collection much easier.

The staff in the department were organized by geographical regions, depending on where the customer lived. Four telephone teams of six people were set up, each supported by two administrative staff to handle paperwork and letters. This structure gave rise to healthy competition between the teams as each tried to beat the performance of the others. Customers without telephones were passed to a specialized 'correspondence team'.

Significant changes were also made to the back office. Selling repossessed properties had previously been carried out by estate agents all over the country. We chose to pass all this work to our own estate agent subsidiary, because we found that their rates of recovery were significantly better than the rates achieved by third parties. In simple terms, the faster we disposed of properties, the better the price achieved. Cases which led to litigation with our customers were administered by a separate section, as were the eventual sales of property and claims from our insurers. Litigation was undertaken by one solicitors' practice, rather than the ninety-two partnerships around the country that we had previously used. These changes resulted in reduced provisioning for bad debts and significant productivity gains, and allowed the arrears teams to focus single-mindedly on collecting missed mortgage subscriptions.

Achievements

Overall, the results speak for themselves. Figure 5.1 shows how Britannia's arrears position improved by comparison with the target that we had set ourselves. The overall market also improved during this period, but we know from our competitors' annual reports that Britannia's performance was substantially better than theirs.

The Society is extremely proud of its re-engineered arrears collec-

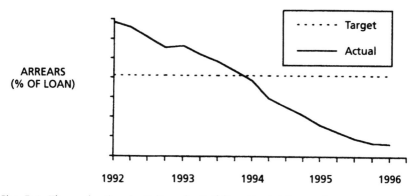

Fig. 5.1 The reduction in Britannia Building Society's mortgage arrears.

tions process. We know that it represents the industry's best practice. In spite of these achievements, the Society is not resting on its laurels. The arrears strategy is reviewed annually to take into account the dynamics of the industry and the economy and the targets are adjusted to ensure that the progress since 1992 will continue.

Extending re-engineering to other areas

Having successfully changed the way we collected mortgage arrears, Britannia has become more ambitious, and we are currently redesigning our lending processes. The scope of this exercise extends from our first contact with a potential borrower in any of our distribution channels to the time the customer makes their first repayment of the loan, and includes all of the business activities in between. We estimate that the jobs of up to 1,700 staff will be affected. Sales staff will have access to a modern point of sale system; underwriting staff will obtain automated access to credit information; sales administrators will be able to electronically enquire about the status of a loan (Has the house been valued? Have employers' references been received?), and so forth.

The Society has established a department specializing in business process re-engineering, which acts as the focal point for radical change within the business and leads the cross-functional effort which is required. Specific skills have been developed within the team covering organization, communications, process analysis and programme management, to complement the Society's existing systems development and project management capabilities. These new competencies will be used increasingly to the Society's advantage as we learn that change is not an event, but more a way of life.

CHAPTER SIX

Managing innovation Part 1: Policies and products

Brian Fries, formerly Vice President, Project and Quality Management, Chemical Bank

Introduction

Chemical Bank and Chase Manhattan merged in 1996 to form Chase Bank. This chapter explains how Chemical UK developed its business and management processes to secure its future as a major constituent of a global financial institution and significant business in its own right. In order to achieve its mission and goals, it developed its own methodology, focused on customer service, personal accountability and clear controls.

In order to improve continuously and embrace the sweeping changes occurring in the financial services industry, the bank recognized the need for constant retraining of its workforce and consistent reinforcement of its values-driven culture. We aim to improve both individual performance and teamwork, through striking the right balance between task-orientation and the motivational aspects of staff performance.

The corporation

Prior to the merger, Chemical Banking Corporation was the fourth largest bank holding company in the USA with total assets of

US$185bn. It employed over 40,000 staff in thirty-five countries, divided into domestic and global divisions.

Chemical had a major regional banking franchise in the tri-state area of New York, New Jersey and Connecticut, and a strong presence in Texas through its affiliate Texas Commerce Bank N.A. With over 400 branches in the tri-state area, Chemical led all other banks in serving middle market companies and had the number one market share in both consumer and small business deposits. In addition, Chemical was one of the top performers in mortgage banking, ranked second nationally in student loans and among the world's top bank creditcard issuers.

Globally, Chemical was a leader in the financial markets around the world, and was frequently engaged as adviser, arranger and agent by many of the largest and best-known companies. Chemical also ranked number one in loan syndications. Its client relationships were maintained through specific industry specializations such as media and telecommunications, utilities, energy and chemicals, financial services and transportation.

The bank's operating services business provided corporate and institutional customers world-wide with transaction processing, fiduciary and information services in support of their capital markets, treasury and commercial activities. Specific products included cash management, custody, trusteeship and agency, and trade services. Chemical processed approximately 70,000 funds transfers daily, totalling US$400bn.

With dealing rooms in all the major financial centres, Chemical was a leader in foreign exchange, and was ranked the top interbank trader since 1992 and the world's largest provider of interest rate risk management products. The bank achieved significant growth in the emerging market economies, being among the leading traders of emerging market debt.

At the end of August 1995, Chemical Banking Corporation announced its planned merger with Chase Manhattan Corporation to form Chase, the largest bank in the United States with assets of US$300bn and shareholders' equity of US$20bn.

The model

The attached 'mind map' (Figure 6.1) shows how Chemical Bank in the UK defined its strategy and used it to address the complex issues of managing change, new product innovation, staff motivation, and

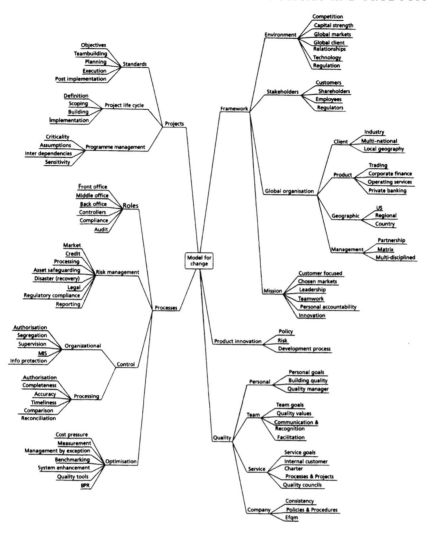

Fig. 6.1 The change process at Chemical Bank UK – a framework for analysis.

process and project control. This chapter examines each of the issues in more detail.

Framework

Environment

During the next few years, it is expected that only eight to ten genuinely global banks will emerge with the ability to offer a broad range of financial services on a truly world-wide scale. The driving forces behind this consolidation come from:

● *Increased competition* – not only from the traditional financial institutions but also from new entrants into the financial intermediary process, for example General Motors with their successful credit card, or Microsoft through its introduction of home banking software and on-line services.

● *Capital strength* – which is necessary to support the businesses and markets in which banks operate. It was lack of capital that brought down Barings, who were unable to absorb the losses created by a rogue trader.

● *Global markets* – operating around the clock in the key money centres demands a reach and presence, where only the largest institutions can successfully compete and maintain management control.

● *Global clients* – who are facing equally complex challenges in their own businesses, demand large banking partners with the ability to deliver the services needed to finance their own worldwide growth and capital needs. Examples of other global industry consolidations include not only the traditional manufacturing industries (e.g. aircraft and motor manufacturing) which went through their consolidations in the eighties, but also more recently high-tech industries such as communications (technology driven) and pharmaceuticals (to be able to support research and development of new drugs).

● *Technology* – which is not only changing markets but is also responsible for their creation. New customer delivery services, for example virtual and home banking through the Internet, are becoming more practical and widely used. Advances in technology are affecting every aspect of our working lives. The cost structures of the industry are being turned upside down. Just keeping up with these changes demands huge levels of investment.

● *Regulation* – while barriers are being relaxed, particularly for global banking, regulation is at the same time becoming more complex, for example in the development of more sophisticated regulatory reporting systems. The Basle directive on market risk measurement and reporting had to be implemented by the end of 1997. This was the inevitable response to the much publicized debacles, frauds and losses, that have hit certain financial institutions and their customers in the recent past.

Stakeholders

Customers

These trends, together with greater demands from the stakeholders of financial institutions are forcing through change at an ever increasing pace. The critical stakeholders for any institution are, first, its customers. They are becoming more sophisticated in their use of financial services, more discerning, willing, and above all, able to shop around for the best deal. This is a revolution for financial services, where until only a very short time ago, both personal and corporate customers were content to be loyal to their banks, like they were to their doctors. Now, very often the customers are challenging the integrity and creditworthiness of the banks they do business with! More competition means that financial services are being treated like any other commodity, and this has had a fundamental effect on the way banks do business.

Stockholders

With increasing competition for their investment funds, shareholders are demanding more satisfactory returns on their investments and they are prepared to take the necessary actions where management is not delivering them. In the seventies and eighties there was continuous preservation of jobs in financial services, which were sheltered from the recessions and rationalization sweeping the manufacturing sectors. In the nineties, downsizing has arrived in financial services and this is seen as the decade for returning real value to the shareholder. This emphasizes the need to maximize revenue and also puts pressure onto reducing operating costs and overheads.

Employees

Forced to adopt leaner, flatter organizations, the banks have changed the working contracts between themselves and their employees. This has had a profound effect on the working lives of staff at all levels. No longer are financial services seen as offering a 'job for life' where the employer provides full security. New contracts, usually unwritten, call for flexibility from the workforce, the ability to adapt rapidly to changing market conditions, and a higher level of knowledge with the need for constant re-education. This requires a new breed of employees, more accountable for their own actions and the success of the corporations they work for, and responsible for the progress and direction of their own careers.

Regulators

The regulators are taking more interest in the detail of all banking activities. This follows a period of extensive deregulation which was intended to make the financial markets freer and more competitive, to increase overall economic activity and to minimize other negative factors such as the fall-out from the oil price shock and developing countries' debt crises.

Global organization

To cope with the new environment and take full advantage of market opportunities, global banks require global organizations which will meet the needs of all their stakeholders. They must be able to provide a full service to their customers and operate effectively in all the key global market locations within the Americas, Europe and the Far East.

Organizations are becoming more complex. On the one hand, efficient service demands that they become leaner, flatter and simpler. On the other, the multi-disciplinary support needs of global clients, international products and differing geographic regions demands a sophisticated global service matrix. Modern executives have to work together in partnership; communicating continually and reaching common decisions. The old hierarchical structures of command and control management are no longer applicable.

Mission

In order to hold together an organization of this scale, it is important for it to have a clear and consistent mission, vision and values throughout the world. The communication of these three beacons is one of the most important tasks of senior management and is what leadership is all about: 'walking the talk', leading by example all the time, every time.

The Chemical Bank Mission statement was as follows:

> ● Our mission is to be the best broad-based financial institution, a leader in our chosen markets.
>
> ● We value the highest ethical standards and leadership, excellence and quality in everything we do while creating and maintaining mutually valuable customer relationships.
>
> ● We are committed to an environment marked by teamwork, accountability, innovation, openness and empowerment that provides an opportunity for personal challenge and growth.

All human resource policies and procedures, including staff selection, performance review, training and remuneration must support the corporation's mission, vision and values.

In order to achieve this mission, we set out the following operating principles:

● *Client focus* – relationship banking is the hallmark of the business. Critical to the success of an institution is its client focus, product excellence and superior execution and service.

● *Global organization* – biased towards organizing business along global lines, establishing centres of expertise and making the most of economies of scale, whether by client, industry, product or staff. This was balanced by local expertise, integration and leadership through strong country managers close to individual market-places.

● *Leverage strength and leadership positions* – using common platforms to drive many products throughout a global network, being a leader in technology and operations to ensure product excellence and best practices execution.

● *Leadership and teamwork* – this is essential for seamless delivery of global capabilities to clients. It demands flexibility in approach and the creation of teams which marshall resources from different areas. Mutual dependencies and partnerships are now a key requirement for any successful integrated financial institution.

● *Focus on results* – this requires measurement systems to identify profits and returns not only by business but by client, product and geography. Performance review and reward were geared to assessing everyone's contributions to overall corporate profitability, and their success in building effective co-operation, responsiveness and teamwork.

● *People are any institution's most important resource* – they are clearly the key to the long-term success of the business. It is not only necessary to have the best people but to create an environment that allows them to maximize their effectiveness, expertise and skills and encourages them to grow and change with the business.

● *Strong risk management* – this covers all aspects of market, credit and operational risk. Proper risk management and control was built into the principles of all our core business strategies and performance measurement systems.

Model for managing change

In Chemical Bank UK we adopted the Burke Litwin model (Figure 6.2) to drive change throughout the institution. It has wide application, whether for individual projects or for wholesale structural change.

The model emphasizes both the 'hard' (on the left side of the model) and the 'soft' (right) aspects of achieving high-level performance. While many managers focus exclusively on achieving the 'hard' task-related issues, it is estimated that 70 per cent of management initiatives fail because of a lack of attention to, or appreciation of the 'softer' aspects of implementing change. It is in fact these 'soft' issues, dealing with people, winning them over, that are more difficult to manage.

Any change process needs to be formulated from a clear vision and translated into a mission statement, or a set of clear concise objectives. For the processes, this can then be translated into more detailed formal strategies, specific and achievable goals and finally to individual task levels, managed through good process and project management disciplines.

The right side of the model indicates that the consistent values of an organization or team should reinforce the day-to-day work practices, both formal and informal, and lead to the establishment of a working climate in which everyone should feel comfortable. This should enable everyone, at all levels, to perform of their best.

Both sides of the model contribute equally to the performance and achievement of the team or organization as a whole. The hard and soft factors within an organization are bound together and are constantly reinforced by the visible application of consistent policies and systems. Each organization will achieve its own balance; successful ones will achieve the right balance, most suitable for their environment.

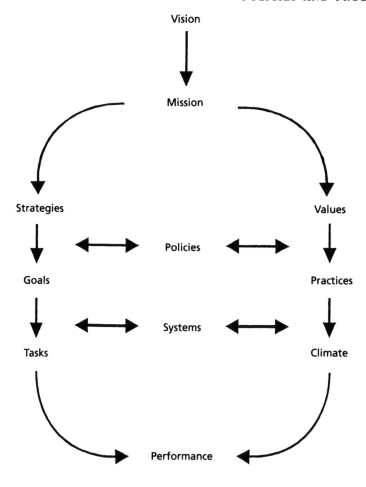

Adapted from the Burke-Litwin management model

Fig. 6.2 Model for managing change.

Considering the model in terms of the top half and the bottom half is also important. It allows senior management to focus on overall direction through creating the vision, setting strategy, defining policy and reinforcing, through their example, the corporation's values. Continually communicating all these is vital for successfully achieving the mission.

While concentrating on the top half of the model, senior managers must whenever necessary also get involved in the application and accomplishment of specific tasks or dealing with issues contributing to the day-to-day working climate of their staff. However, they must be able to distinguish between the two types of activity and hence keeping the 'helicopter' perspective is vitally important. It is all too easy to get lost in the detail at the bottom of the model, to be working ever harder but losing sight of the overall direction – crisis management.

The task of management is to keep the balance between left and right, top and bottom.

Product innovation

In a highly competitive environment, product strategy and new product development are critical. Chemical developed a new product approval process adopting a multi-disciplined approach to meet the needs and requirements of all interested parties and stakeholders. Whilst speed is critical, rushing poorly thought out or badly implemented ideas into the market-place can lead to disaster.

A new product policy was created:

- to facilitate the timely assessment and approval of new products;
- to ensure that the risks associated with each new product are identified, analysed and managed prior to introduction; and
- to define clear responsibility and accountability.

Defining the types of new product as 'full', 'limited variation of an existing product' or 'a one-time transaction', the policy required that a sponsor or developer set out a clear description of the product, its features, customer benefits and target markets. For full new product proposals, financial information, effects on the corporation's financial statements and ratios (e.g. income and expense, profit margins, return on equity, assets and risk adjusted capital) for an appropriate time horizon were required. In addition, it was necessary to establish start-up costs, develop product pricing schedules, identify sources of funding and set out the detailed assumptions made on volumes, revenue and expense projections. Where a new product required major capital investment, the necessary capital investment procedures also had to be completed.

One of the key components of the new product approval process was to identify and analyse all associated product risks. These include credit, market, accounting, tax, legal and regulatory as well as operational and systems risks. This process required the

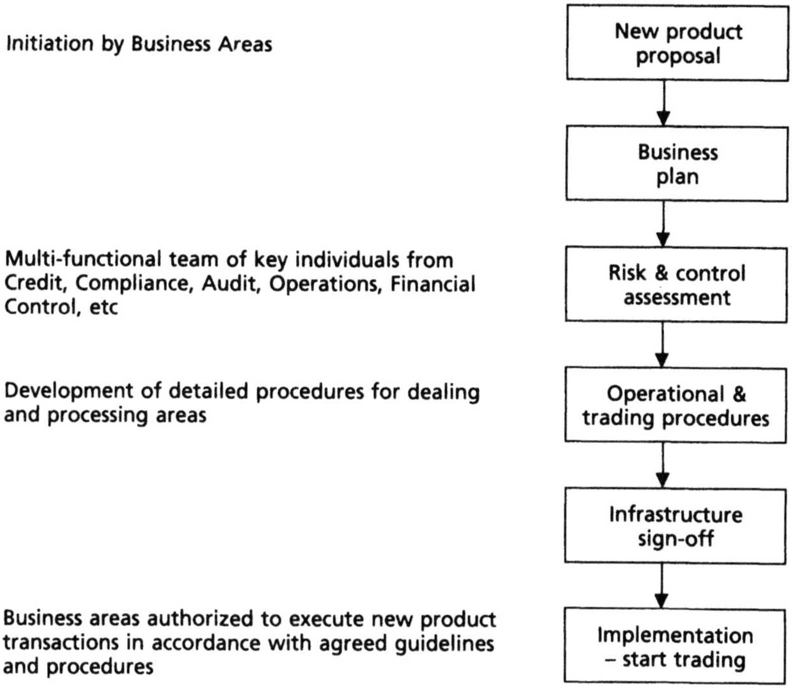

Initiation by Business Areas

```
┌─────────────────┐
│   New product   │
│    proposal     │
└─────────────────┘
         │
         ▼
┌─────────────────┐
│    Business     │
│      plan       │
└─────────────────┘
         │
         ▼
```

Multi-functional team of key individuals from
Credit, Compliance, Audit, Operations, Financial
Control, etc

```
┌─────────────────┐
│  Risk & control │
│    assessment   │
└─────────────────┘
         │
         ▼
```

Development of detailed procedures for dealing
and processing areas

```
┌─────────────────┐
│  Operational &  │
│trading procedures│
└─────────────────┘
         │
         ▼
┌─────────────────┐
│  Infrastructure │
│    sign-off     │
└─────────────────┘
         │
         ▼
```

Business areas authorized to execute new product
transactions in accordance with agreed guidelines
and procedures

```
┌─────────────────┐
│ Implementation  │
│ – start trading │
└─────────────────┘
```

Fig. 6.3 Streamlining the process.

involvement and sign-off of the key functional support areas, including auditing.

Considerable effort was put into streamlining the process (Figure 6.3), for example through regionalization, the use of groupware technology (Lotus Notes) and suitable operating statistics to track the progress and timeliness of all product proposals from initiation through to implementation.

Successful product innovation prospers only if the culture of the organization is right, supportive of new initiatives and has the appetite for taking on new, but measured risk. In the capital markets area, for example, our financial engineering group was constantly creating new ideas and scouring the markets for trends or new possibilities. Examples include UK 'gilt repos',[1] emerging market securities, cross currency swaps and other specialized variations of derivative products.

---

[1] A repo is an agreement to buy (sell) a security while at the same time agreeing to sell (buy) the same security at a predetermined future date. The price at which the reverse transaction takes place determines the interest rate over the period.

These ideas were then brainstormed with teams of dealers, sales and marketing staff to develop the basics of a new product. A small team of key people, including Controllers, Operations, Credit and Market Risk and Compliance staff, would then work together to formalize the new product proposal. Flexibility and speed must be balanced by the appropriate controls and checks. To get this right demands the highest levels of commitment and teamwork from all parties with innovation at the top of the priority list.

Quality

In order to prepare staff to cope with the new culture demanded by an increasingly competitive environment, Chemical introduced a quality programme to give all staff the ability to face these new challenges and achieve greater success for themselves and their teams as well as the company. The programme was called 'The Chemical Equation', defined as:

Personal quality + Team quality + Service quality = Company quality

Its overall objectives being to:

- consistently meet, or exceed, customer expectations;
- generate employee pride and commitment;
- emphasize quality as being synonymous with control;
- continuously improve and learn;
- embrace change.

At the outset, the programme needed complete senior management commitment to demonstrate that this would not be a one-off event which would be forgotten as soon as a new fad or an alternative management guru became fashionable. We achieved this through off-site high-level management meetings, subsequent publicity through staff magazines, presentations by the senior management and their own attendance and participation in staff training courses. For us it was a prerequisite that managers must be seen to lead by example.

For the next preparatory stage, we gave middle managers the skills to introduce the programme as partners with their staff, develop action plans for continuous improvement and maintain the quality initiative's momentum. All managers attended quality workshops based around the themes of external and internal customer service, staff motivation and delegation, team building, communication, and goal setting. These were constructed around five key work areas:

- staff and team development;
- customer focus and communication;
- core processes;
- projects;
- personal and professional development.

Also, a 'Quality values questionnaire' was sent to 1,000 key staff to get them to rate their teams and/or departments on a set of quality criteria encompassing:

- goal setting;
- effectiveness and efficiency;
- implementation;
- ownership and accountability;
- delegation;
- decision-making;
- quality awareness;
- control awareness;
- our department's communication;
- inter-departmental communication;
- customer focus;
- creativity and innovation;
- commitment;
- recognition;
- employee development;
- psychological environment.

The initial results were very good. Through the personal involvement and encouragement of the departmental managers, an overall response rate of 80 per cent was achieved. Departmental opinions varied widely, but consistently high scores were reported for customer focus, commitment, control awareness and effectiveness and efficiency. This gave the bank a sound basis to build on strengths in these areas and then focus on addressing weaker scores. Not surprisingly, these included communication, delegation, employee development and recognition. Aspects of the quality programme and training were then specifically tailored and given greater emphasis to address these issues.

We repeated the survey at regular intervals and it was important that staff should rate their teams, not themselves individually. When the results were analysed, they discussed them together in small groups and established joint action plans encompassing management and staff, to deal with the issues which they agreed should have highest priority. This process formed the basis for regular team meetings at which quality issues were discussed openly and a process of continuous improvement established. Each subsequent survey provided important measures for management of how staff perceptions of their own performance and the organization's effectiveness were changing, both departmentally and throughout the bank as a whole.

We launched a bank-wide programme of individual 'Building quality' workshops, covering personal attitudes and the service quality aspects of staff performance. The objectives were to make everyone realise that they each make a unique contribution and a real difference to the working environment; for themselves, those around them, their internal customers and ultimately the external customers as well.

We placed great emphasis on customer service, both internally and externally, and stressed the importance of the way products were delivered, not just the quality of the products themselves. As a result of gathering the managers' views during their workshops, we established a 'customer charter' to cover those criteria that managers considered most important in receiving good service from each other. The ten key areas identified were:

- professional competence;
- honesty and integrity;
- accessibility and responsiveness;
- courtesy;
- open communication and feedback;
- completeness and accuracy;
- timeliness;
- commitment to service quality;
- value for money;
- user friendliness.

To implement the charter, individual managers met with their customers and discussed specifically what level of service should be provided under each heading, and how it should be measured; the relative importance and any trade-offs between areas were also agreed. Very often, the relationship between different areas (e.g. completeness and accuracy and timeliness of information versus value for money) come sharply into focus. Typically, this process led to a clearer understanding of customer needs and ensured perceptions match realities.

The process was supplemented with regular reappraisals of actual performance and service quality through the use of balanced score cards, completed by both supplier and customer (Figure 6.4).

The use of 'score cards' helped break down communication barriers between groups and departments. Open discussion of the key issues led to the development of joint action plans for continuous improvement of both internal and external services and products. We found that this improved inter-departmental teamwork, especially in the areas of product innovation and systems development.

We then introduced an ongoing quality strategy under the Chemical Equation banner, called 'Striking the Balance'. This supported the overall commitment to both hard and soft issues. For each element of the Chemical Equation, the strategy established overall goals and measures of success. These were tailored by individual staff members, their teams and/or departments to be specific, challenging and demonstrate a commitment to continuous improvement. In summary, the generic goals (Figure 6.5) were:

● *Personal quality* – all staff embrace the objectives and practices of the Chemical Equation and take responsibility for their own personal and professional development.

● *Team quality* – link individual goals to shared team goals through common values and strategies. Realize success through teamwork and celebrate achievements together.

● *Service quality* – be customer-focused – deliver high-quality internal service to ensure excellent external quality service. Meet today's expectations, continuously seeking improvement and providing innovative solutions.

● *Company quality* – develop our values and culture through the Chemical Equation, involving everyone throughout the bank. Ensure long-term success by embracing the objectives and practices of the Chemical Equation.

CHEMICAL BANK UK – INTERNAL CUSTOMER CHARTER

DEPT:	**Foreign Exchange Operations**				
CUSTOMER:	*Global Trading Division*				
DATE/PERIOD/PROJECT:	*Up to 30 October 1995*				
EVALUATED BY:	*Tom Smith, John Brown*				

Area	Weighting	% Customer Score	% Supplier Score	Weighted Cust/Supp Gap	Weighted Ave/Ideal Gap
Professional Competence	13	75	70	0.7	3.6
Honesty & Integrity	8	70	75	0.4	2.2
Accessibility & Responsiveness	12	80	80	0.0	2.4
Courtesy	8	75	80	0.4	1.8
Open Communication & Feedback	10	70	60	1.0	3.5
Completeness & Accuracy	11	85	75	1.1	2.2
Timeliness	11	85	80	0.5	1.9
Commitment to Service Quality	10	75	90	1.5	1.8
Value for Money	7	70	60	0.7	2.5
User Friendliness	10	75	80	0.5	2.3
Weighted Totals out of 100	100	76.6	75.4		

PRIORITY AREAS FOR IMPROVEMENT ARE INDICATED BY THE FOLLOWING MAXIMUM

Maximum Customer/Supplier Gap __1.5__ Commitment to Service Quality
(Target is 0)

Maximum Average/Ideal Gap __3.6__ Professional competence
(Target is 0)

Overall Average Weighted Total Score __76.0__ Previous period __74.8__
(Target is 100)

Fig. 6.4 Example of internal customer charter.

STRIKING THE BALANCE – THE ENABLERS

Personal Quality
➤ **Smart Personal Goals** cover all key work and developmental areas and assist each employee in realizing their full potential

➤ **Personal Development Plans** help employees identify their developmental needs and encourage them to define specific action plans with completion dates

➤ **Competency Based Performance Reviews** help employees compare their actual performance against their defined competencies and review progress towards achieving their goals and personal development plans

Team Quality
➤ **Smart Team Goals** assist teams to work together. The goals must be accepted by everyone and be consistent with corporate goals and business objectives

➤ **Quality Values Survey** is a periodic survey, completed by staff, relating to sixteen key aspects of the working climate. The action plans resulting from the surveys allow everyone to work together to improve motivation and performance

➤ **Open Communication**, appropriate and timely, is the cornerstone of a Quality organization

Service Quality
➤ **Smart Service Goals** need to be customer focused and encompass measurable improvements

➤ **Internal Customer Charter** enables managers to mutually agree, with their customers, service levels in ten key areas. Regular completion of score cards allows both customers and suppliers to review performance and implement action plans for improvements.

➤ **Quality Tools** are measurement and problem solving techniques to control and continuously improve processes.

Company Quality
➤ **Consistency of Purpose** is achieved through the Chemical Equation programme. It is co-ordinated by the Project and Quality Management group, provides common training and helps departments implement their own Quality initiatives.

➤ **Communication** demonstrates the commitment of management to the Chemical Equation and the importance that the culture, values and climate have in enabling the Bank to achieve its goals

➤ **Building Quality** is a training programme of one-day workshops and team sessions to make employees aware of the Chemical Equation, generate positive personal attitudes and improve personal service to their customers

➤ **Managing Quality** is a methodology to assist managers in setting goals and concentrating on their key work areas

➤ **Recognition** is the way we encourage each other

➤ **Process and Project Management** ensures that core business processes are well controlled, effective and efficient and that projects are completed successfully on time

➤ **Team Facilitation** assists the establishment of effective teams, enabling them to adopt common values and strategies, and work together towards shared goals.

➤ **Quality Councils** offer the opportunity for staff to be involved in the solution of departmental or team issues and improve processes. They play a primary role in the Awards for Quality scheme.

➤ **Benchmarking** is the objective comparison of processes against other world class organizations to establish best practice.

➤ **Defined Processes and Procedures** provide the disciplines and best practices to ensure overall consistency, effectiveness and control of all key activities.

➤ **Investors In People (IIP)** is a national standard which pulls together aspects of personal and team development as a means of achieving corporate goals.

➤ **European Foundation Quality Model (EFQM)** provides a framework to measure ourselves against a set of Quality criteria applied to leading European organizations

Fig. 6.5 The quality strategy.

In order to achieve the goals and objectives of the strategy, a series of 'enablers', tools and training were used. These included personal development planning and competency-based appraisals to support staff; the quality values surveys and team facilitation assisted team-building. The customer charters and departmental quality councils also contributed to improved service quality. In addition, defined process and project management standards provided the disciplines and best practices to be followed. These ensured overall consistency, effectiveness and control of all key activities.

Summary

This chapter has addressed how Chemical Bank UK set the strategic framework for managing change in a fast-moving environment. We put great emphasis on achieving the right balance – managing not only the task-oriented issues but also dealing up-front with the people aspects – the values, working practices and the climate of the organization. The practical application of this framework gave us not only a successful model but also the ability to achieve consistently our business goals.

CHAPTER SEVEN

Managing innovation
Part 2: Processes

Brian Fries, formerly Vice President,
Project and Quality Management,
Chemical Bank

In Chapter 6 we introduced Chemical's strategic framework. Two critical elements of that framework were our approaches to managing business processes and to running the projects through which we delivered strategic change and achieved our business objectives. These are explained in greater detail in this chapter.

Processes

Roles

Processes which are critical to the successful operation of the businesses need to be efficient, reliable, robust and well controlled. In addition, they must provide a high-quality service to customers that will differentiate us from the competition.

We defined an operational model for each of our major businesses to act as a framework to ensure the above goals were met. For example, there was a generic model for derivatives processing (Figure 7.1). It had three main operational areas: front office, middle office and back office. The processes performed by these areas were

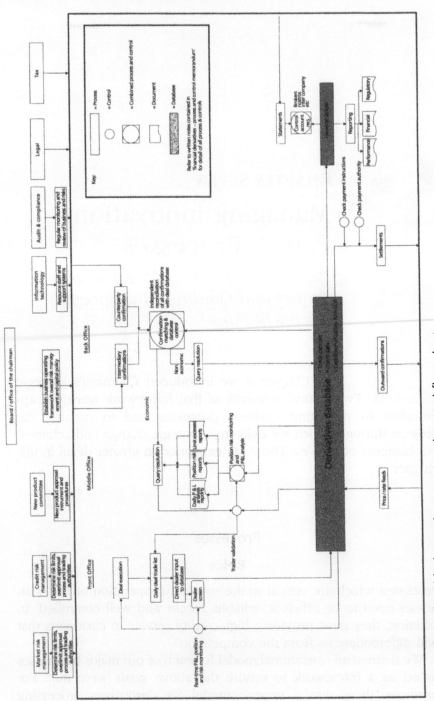

Fig. 7.1 Derivatives ideal generic process and control flow chart.

supported by other management and support functions providing the facilities and expertise required to perform the necessary operations effectively, to control and report on them.

● *Front office* – involved in deal execution and initial data capture such that trade details were input directly to the main operational systems. A central database acted as the source of information used by all areas.

● *Middle office* – had three main functions: first, to provide an independent point of calculation of the profits and losses made by the traders on a daily basis. The second function was the production of management information, monitoring of trading limits and investigation of excesses. Finally, the area provided a central resource for the resolution of queries arising on trades – communicating between the front and back offices.

● *Back office* – had the functions of the production and matching of trade confirmations, settlements and nostro account reconciliation.

The key support functions for these roles included Information Technology to provide system support and the computer operations, Credit and Market Risk to ensure appropriate counterparty and trading limits were established and adhered to, Controllers for accounting and reporting, and Legal and Compliance to ensure regulations were complied with. In addition, Auditing performed ongoing independent reviews of the integrity of operations generally and reported any exceptions within the processes to senior management.

Risk management

Strong risk management formed part of the bank's culture and was built into our core business strategies and performance measurement systems. The proper measurement of risk versus reward in all business activities and a focus on internal control contributed to the daily acceptance and subsequent management of risk.

The broad nature of the bank's activities and their diversification assisted in this process. The bank's ability to counterbalance downturns in particular markets or economies was based on a wide range of products with varied income streams deriving from interest margins, fees and trading results across all geographic regions and major currencies. Strong global management disciplines allowed both opportunities and threats to be identified quickly, and resources to be diverted to achieve the best returns.

Chemical defined risk within eight broad categories:

- *Market risk* – resultant from a change in the value of proprietary positions including related hedging and capital allocations. This can arise from market movements in currencies, interest rates, equities or commodities, as well as investment assets such as real estate or venture capital funds.

- *Credit risk* – arising from a counterparty's inability to pay an obligation when due, including the failure of clearing and settlement activities. Credit risk also includes the risk that related collateral may not be adequate.

- *Processing risk* – arising from a failure of the processes in the operations or data processing areas, manual or automated, to operate as intended. This risk relates to the failure to record transactions and/or the inability to provide meaningful management information to permit proper monitoring of business activities.

- *Asset safeguarding* – due to the improper acts of employees, customers or third parties such as fraud, theft, the concealment of trades, destruction of records, conflict of interests, misuse of position or other misrepresentation.

- *Disaster recovery* – the risk of loss arising from the inability of the business and/or support operations to recover from a disruption through power loss, fire, flood, terrorist attack, etc. The development of global markets, sophistication of automated systems and the concentration of support operations have significantly increased these risks in recent years.

- *Legal risk* – loss arising from civil penalties or damages, generally as a result of failure to meet a contractual obligation or deemed duty.

- *Regulatory compliance* – loss caused by non-compliance with laws and regulations, including, for example, insider trading. Given the global nature and complexity of the bank's activities, these regulations are extensive and are enforced through a myriad of regulatory bodies.

- *Reporting risk* – the effect of inaccurately prepared financial statements or published regulatory reports, which should reflect the institution's financial position accurately, fairly and in accordance with all disclosure requirements.

Control

In order to manage risk effectively and to ensure the smooth operation of processes, strong internal controls are paramount. Controls should be designed into processes primarily to safeguard the assets of the institution and its customers, ensure the reliability of financial records, establish compliance with applicable laws and regulations, ensure the business is conducted in accordance with management's stated objectives and to foster operational efficiency.

Much has been written about the inefficiencies of controls – that they kill initiative and go against the very ethos of the modern downsized, re-engineered, super efficient organization. How can you empower staff but not stifle them through overbearing levels of control and perceived bureaucracy?

The well-publicized names that have had weak controls have suffered accordingly. Good control is an integral part of effective processes. Build it automatically into the systems and processes from the outset. Allow staff to act within clear boundaries in an enlightened way, understanding and respecting the control processes that not only help them get the job done effectively, but also protect them as well.

Control is fundamental to the whole operating environment. Management sets the tone, by emphasizing constantly that integrity and control are a critical part of the values of the institution. They must build it into all the corporation's policies and procedures and above all reward those managers who maintain well controlled operations. Those who are lax should be penalized and should be seen to be so treated.

The operation of control is important at two levels. First, supervisory controls exercised by management provide the basic framework and monitor effectively the operation of basic processing controls. These supervisory controls include daily hands-on management review of activities, adequate segregation of duties, data security and contingency planning; appropriate operational management information, speedy highlighting and escalation of errors and exceptions, independent proofing and regular verification of assets.

A basic set of processing controls should operate over all transactions to ensure they are properly authorized, completely and accurately processed and reported in an accurate and timely manner. For example, transactions should only be originated by designated individuals operating within specified limits of authority. All transactions should be independently verified and confirmed as early as possible.

All transactions must be recorded in the books of account on a timely basis and agreed back to underlying records. The carrying value of assets must be measured against current market prices and adjusted at appropriate frequency.

In order to ensure controls over operations are appropriate in all areas, we developed an internal control matrix to be applied to each product. It was developed by using a library of generic risks and control objectives and suitably tailoring them to a particular situation. For each stage of processing, appropriate control objectives to mitigate risks were identified and recorded to ensure they were appropriately included within the daily operating procedures. These controls could be physical, procedural, or embedded in the bank's information and processing systems.

Each control matrix covered a product, or group of products with similar processing cycles. The matrices were organized by control phases throughout the trade's life cycle, from deal creation, through deal capture, processing, settlement and the accounting functions.

In any banking transaction process it is important to segregate duties, or the tasks that an employee is able to carry out. This ensures that an individual is not able to act alone in committing a fraud. An example of the product control matrix related to this issue is shown in Table 7.1.

Table 7.1 A product control matrix

Objective	Control
Access to account creation processing is restricted to authorized personnel, segregated from incompatible duties.	The deal making functions are adequately segregated from those relating to: • risk management • deal accounting, including reconciliation of the general ledger • deal confirmation • settlement of mature deals. User access rights are restricted to only those processing functions and data files required for users' normal duties. User access rights are: • pre-approved by management • based only on written authorization, which is retained as an audit trail, and matched against reported changes to access rights by the security administrator.

A control matrix also has value as a reference document which, when used in conjunction with departmental operating procedures, can help train employees as to how the control structure is integrated into the organization's *modus operandi*. This leads to a deeper understanding of the products involved, necessary control objectives, and the mechanisms which ensure effective controls are achieved.

Optimization

Once processes have been established, they need regular reappraisal. In a complex, ever changing environment, even the most effective processes must change; in order to adapt to new requirements, they are always added to, enhanced with a new report here, a PC solution there. End-user computing has revolutionized the ability of newly skilled knowledge workers to be flexible and respond to all sorts of *ad hoc* information demands – great for one-off reports, but highly inefficient if the whole reporting system relies on these personally developed spreadsheets every time.

When the business evolves and associated operations are no longer key to achieving core business objectives, the processes often fail to adapt, and live on regardless. They become highly ineffective and consume valuable resources better employed elsewhere. Some processes continue just because they have always been done that way, no longer questioned, failing to make use of new technology or new applications used elsewhere in the bank.

In order to identify and overcome these situations, we instituted a constant review process of optimization. In order to be objective, it was independent and carried out by personnel trained in process control, but aware of the business, its drivers and needs. The designated teams focused on whole business units or operating departments, breaking their review down into the following categories:

- product profitability analysis;
- client analysis;
- productivity analysis and best practice implementation;
- expense rationalization and unit costing;
- internal/external benchmarking;
- operations and technology re-engineering.

Through such a wide-ranging review, it is possible to ensure all processes match critical core business needs, continue to meet customer requirements and expectations, reflect best practice and are highly efficient. Typical areas often highlighted for process improvement include the identification of non-value added tasks, rekeying of data into multiple systems or PCs; redundant or duplicated data, high ratios of checking and/or reworking and obvious disconnects especially at departmental and functional boundaries.

It is first necessary to identify the key products, the unit's customer profile, volumes and values of transactions. These can be aligned against the systems and processes, staff employed and the costs to ensure that resources are being applied to the most effective activities in the best possible way.

We employed a standard methodology to model the core processes. Before starting, it is necessary to define the objectives and boundaries of the processes, the initial inputs and final outputs and the interactions with customers. Charting is then used to record individual or groups of activities, their inputs, outputs, staff roles, systems used, etc. Depending on the perceived objectives of the review, for example to try to reduce resources consumed, reduce process cycle times, estimate the effects of higher volumes, relevant metrics need to be captured. This is usually done through interviewing the staff involved in the actual processes.

Typical metrics gathered include elapsed times for individual activities and the process as a whole; defined start and finish times and any deadlines for outputs; peak and average volumes processed; capacity restraints within the process; levels and effects of errors and reworks required; resourcing levels, skills required and associated cost data. Once we collected this data and recorded it in the model, computer simulation allowed us to perform a cause and effect analysis to help identify inefficiencies or process bottlenecks and point to possible improvements.

Box 7.1 Modelling securities settlements

As a pilot project for process modelling and redesign, we chose to model some of the processes of the securities settlements department. This department processed securities bought and sold on behalf of the bank. They provided dealer support, liaised with the back-offices of counterparty institutions and ensured that securities were settled correctly and on time.

The modelling methodology consisted of six steps:

- project definition;
- initial analysis;

- definition of critical business process;
- redesign of critical business process;
- impact analysis;
- implementation.

We used a PC application which has a front-end looking much like any flowcharting or mapping tool. But behind this lies a powerful database for recording the metrics of the processes drawn onto the map together with a powerful rule writer for analysis. For example: 'What happens if I have two people performing this part of the process, does the overall process improve?', or 'If I centre the process around the tasks themselves rather than the people who perform the process, will it become more effective?'

The settlements process was initially modelled not by interview or observation of the staff, but from departmental procedures. Whilst this meant that staff weren't disturbed from their work, it made understanding the process more difficult, there were greater initial inaccuracies and the department involved felt little ownership of the modelling which we were performing.

Once the process was modelled, though, we got the opportunity to work with the department's Quality Council. This meant that we had a group of people in the department who were committed to making changes for the better and whom we could 'bounce our ideas off.' We continued the process through opportunity workshops with the Quality Council and estimated productivity improvements of some 30 per cent were achieved.

The key lesson from this exercise was that the buy-in of those involved in change is crucial. Staff must feel that they are making change happen, rather than change being something which is 'done to them'. If they don't, you are doomed to failure – or at best, only limited success.

Box 7.2 Derivatives trading quality and process improvements

The quality and process improvements initiative was established to improve existing control procedures; our goal was to implement new preventative measures to reduce the risk of losses arising from incomplete, inaccurate, spurious or missing trade information.

This was largely achieved by identifying critical business processes that were underperforming and setting specific and measurable improvement targets. The key to our success in developing process improvements was constructive communication at all levels through:

- teamwork – cross-functional ownership of the derivatives process;
- quality – high levels of productivity and the eradication of errors;
- project management – better implementation of new ideas in a controlled and timely manner.

The following list contains the significant and specific objectives of our programme:

- dealers' reports – accurate and timely delivery of all reports;
- improved risk management and deal limit monitoring;

- implementation of enhanced dealer position and P&L controls;
- faster query resolution process including tighter control, the prompt identification of exceptions and quicker response times;
- improved communications and teamwork between front/middle/back offices;
- streamlined process for trade confirmations leading to improved timing and delivery with brokers and counterparties;
- improved timeliness of incoming counterparty confirmations;
- enhancements to overall stability and robustness of trading and processing systems.

The underlying business and operational issues fell into four distinct areas:

- team-building;
- process and control;
- MIS;
- technology.

Team-building

We used a combination of creative thinking techniques and open discussion, while encouraging the team to concentrate on the overall process across the various areas, and not just limiting themselves to departmental issues.

In building the team for this programme, we deliberately maintained focus on addressing communication inhibitors between team members and breaking down departmental barriers. Initially we experienced conflict due to protective behaviours and attitudes, but this evolved into a more cohesive and productive group.

Openness is the critical success factor in achieving this; building trust and cooperation throughout the team allowed us to get to the root cause of potential process shortfalls.

By gaining consensus on both the real problem areas and the best course of action, we ensured shared ownership for the process improvements and successful implementation.

Process and Control

We developed jointly a generic process and control flow chart for the derivatives business; this provided an overview of the key controls and processes involved, allowing us to produce a model of 'best practices' to guarantee an objective approach.

This was a key component in our improvement initiative, enabling us to compare the ideal to actual and analyse areas of difference. By examining the reasons why these differences exist, we could decide whether to maintain or redesign our procedures.

MIS Review

We defined the necessary operational reports required to demonstrate the effectiveness of key controls. This included the comprehensive review of MIS in the operational areas on a timely basis and data analysis to identify particular workflow inefficiencies. In addition, we established tracking mechanisms for existing processes and trend analysis against appropriate benchmarks.

Technology
This area is central to derivatives processing and is continually being examined together with technology staff to find ways to enhance existing systems and to introduce new and more productive technology.

Benchmarking

Once these internal analyses have been performed, it may be desirable to consider how the department and its processes compare to known best practice, or to carry out benchmarking comparisons with other areas within the bank, or externally. It is important before embarking on such exercises to define carefully the objectives of the survey and ensure it will be clearly focused. Some of the questions that need to be asked at this stage are:

● What would make the biggest improvements for our customers, to our revenues/profits, etc.?

● What are the core processes that we really want to be good at and which will differentiate us from our competitors?

● What would have the most effect on productivity/staff motivation and satisfaction?

● Is it possible to collect the necessary data, internally or externally? Is it highly sensitive and therefore unlikely to be shared by competitors?

● Have we focused on a small number of issues where we are prepared to implement highlighted areas of improvement?

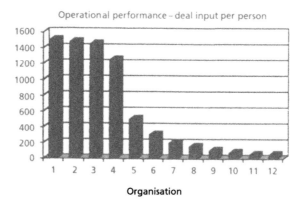

Fig. 7.2 A Treasury benchmarking survey.

Very often, to go outside the organization, it is easier to employ a third party, a trade association or independent consultants to help gather the data from a number of peer group companies. They will report back to all participants on a fully confidential and objective basis.

The results of all benchmarking exercises should be scrutinized critically to ensure the reliability, accuracy and relevance of both the data and the conclusions drawn. Some experience is needed in using this technique effectively, but it is worthwhile as a way of identifying the best and measuring your performance against it.

Box 7.3 A treasury benchmarking survey

In 1995, Chemical Bank took part in a treasury benchmarking survey undertaken by Price Waterhouse. The survey, including thirteen other banks, benchmarked the trading activities of the major participants in the markets in London. Data was collected by a Price Waterhouse analyst from existing MIS sources and through interviews with the managers of the key support and processing areas. The information was submitted in the form of five key schedules – average value and volume of trades by product, headcount, systems functionality, costs (market data, telecoms, brokerage) and errors, and direct costs per trade. The data was collated from all survey participants and any anomalies resolved through references to each bank.

The results of the survey were then published to each bank in the form of a large number of slides (data was not attributable to individual competitors). Information from the previous year's survey was also provided on some slides to examine trends on the year. An example slide is reproduced in Figure 7.2. In addition, we defined a peer group of six banks, more equal in terms of size and market presence, and this allowed data to be reviewed against comparable competitors.

What did we gain from the study? First, it gave us additional insights into the operations of the markets and our group of peer banks in particular. It gave us some crude measurements and benchmarks for overall costings and productivity, against which our ongoing operational MIS and trend data could be compared. Finally, it indicated to us areas where other banks were investing to improve their own system functionality and enabled us to ensure we were maintaining a competitive edge.

Business process re-engineering

All these approaches help to develop better processes and allow for continuous step-by-step improvement. Sometimes this is not enough, and a full re-engineering exercise is necessary. This may be due to the wholly uneconomic cost of current activities, new customer expectations beyond current delivery capabilities, new competition or outdated technology. Such fundamental change requires a dedicated sponsor with the necessary vision, ability to get the commitment from the whole team and the tenacity to persevere even when seemingly insurmountable obstacles are put in the way of the necessary change.

Business re-engineering projects by their nature demand a full re-examination of business strategy, information technology, organizational structure, and the roles of individuals in the development of highly effective and cost efficient processes. They must be customer-focused and take into account both external and internal influences on the environment, in particular the actions of competitors and effects of technological change. It is the time to face up to tough questions – what business are we in? What should we be doing? Are these processes core to achieving our business objectives? Can they be achieved better in-house, or should they be outsourced?

To do the necessary analysis requires small multi-disciplinary teams focused on a new vision for the affected business and defining a clear strategy as to how it should be implemented. As always, sufficient emphasis has to be placed on the people issues involved in the process to ensure success. These include building on the fundamentals of the quality programme, communicating how the proposed changes are likely to affect individuals, and being seen to be fair, even when, because of the effects of rationalization, the news may be bad. Use the principle that there cannot be too much communication, providing it is clear, consistent and open.

Box 7.4 Re-engineering the human resources department

Within the bank, an early use of our process modelling tool was with our Human Resources Department. The HR function was split over three sites and employed twenty-six staff. The aims of the project were threefold:

- to reduce the administrative burden on HR staff;
- to allow HR to better meet the requirements of their customers throughout the bank;
- to reduce costs and allow the department to shrink in size over time.

These objectives were to be achieved via a complete overhaul of the work HR performed and the way this work was done. A new system was to be chosen which would replace a multiplicity of existing spreadsheets and databases. This reduced system input and improved data integrity. In addition, it had automated interfaces to the general ledger and to the payroll which was handled by an external supplier. The new system was to be supported by new policies and procedures for the whole HR department so that a common level of service could be achieved.

We initiated the project at an offsite meeting with the HR department facilitated by internal and external consultants. The objective of the offsite was to get the

---

commitment of the whole department towards the project and for them to realize the differences between what they wanted to do and what their customers wanted of them. Some of the high-level functionality of a new information system was also discussed.

We started by identifying what processes were currently performed and recorded them using a PC-based process modelling system. We looked for similarities between different processes, current use of spreadsheets, databases and for best practice amongst HR staff. The modelling was performed in a series of workshops with staff who were both customers and providers of the services involved. An opportunities log was kept throughout the process so that all new ideas could be recorded and then reviewed collectively.

Overall, the project approach was 'bottom-up'. We reviewed the work currently performed, what customers required and the good ideas of staff to help define what their new system should give them. Through their involvement and participation, this approach gave the staff a greater sense of ownership of the new system which they would have to work in the future.

Projects

Project and change management is key to the success of any business endeavour. Usually, managers have to initiate projects and be responsible to achieve specified objectives on time and within budget, while at the same time managing the operation of their normal core processes. Within a large, complex organization, projects are usually multi-disciplinary and require the use of virtual teams – people with different reporting lines brought together for a specific project on a part-time basis. The management of such projects is difficult. It needs a disciplined approach, both to strategy and task, as well as the people issues, working practices and climate.

As a result, we developed an overall project methodology and standard, supported by a formal system development project life cycle (PLC). The methodology was broken down into the following seven key phases.

1. Define goals

This included setting out business objectives, the scope and terms of reference of the project, identifying the project sponsor and key customers, assessing the level of project risk, its criticality and complexity. This was communicated to all interested parties through the distribution of project impact notification and risk assessment documents.

2. Assign responsibilities

Clear roles and responsibilities, especially project manager and project co-ordinator, were assigned at the outset and full accountability established and communicated. If necessary, a project steering committee was set up including representatives of all interested businesses, technology, operations and support groups, such as Controllers and Auditing.

Applicable corporate policies, standards and procedures (e.g. PLC, new products, etc.) were considered at this stage to ensure they were taken fully into account in project planning.

Where special expertise or resources were needed the participation of internal or external consultants was decided.

3. Establish team

Having set the objectives and scope of the project and appointed a management structure, the next stage was to identify the key members of the team, ensuring they had the correct skill sets and that they would be made available for the project.

Off-site meetings often took place to build the team using a facilitator. The objectives of these meetings was to get the commitment of all the team members to the overall goals of the project and to their individual contributions. They agreed how to measure their success as a team by defining both hard and soft critical success factors and then discussed and established project strategy.

Obviously within any team, the involvement of all parties and open communication based on trust need to be established. The sooner this is done the better, but in some circumstances (e.g. staff based in different locations with different reporting lines), this will take a considerable time. Team-building was a prime responsibility of the project manager.

4. Plan project

Detailed project planning starts with setting out the key milestones within the project. These represent the completion of key deliverables or phases, decision or review points or any other important landmarks within the project. They allow the project manager to break down the whole project into manageable chunks and be in a position to easily measure and demonstrate progress. As a result he can celebrate intermediate successes with his team.

In order to achieve the milestones, the project manager and/or his team had to identify the underlying key tasks, delivery dates, resources and inter-dependencies on other projects or areas outside their control. A detailed plan was then set up on a project-tracking software package (e.g. Microsoft Project).

Costs were estimated and budgeted appropriately, employing a structured methodology, and dependent on the size of the project an expanse tracking system was established within the management accounting system.

As part of the planning process, significant risk factors, worst-case scenarios and resource conflicts were considered and factored into the plan. This required the design of high-level controls and fallback and contingency procedures.

Once the plan was completed and committed to by the team, senior management approval was required and a regular reporting process was put in place. The level and extent of these procedures depended on the size, cost and complexity of the project.

5. Execute project

The more thorough the planning phases of the project, the easier the execution. More projects fail because the scope changes during the life of the project than for any other reason. All unnecessary changes must be avoided, and it is worthwhile establishing very strict control over the acceptance of any changes to the scope or the deliverables of the project. This is one area where it is beneficial to be over-burdensome with bureaucracy!

Establish comprehensive opportunity and problem logs to capture good ideas for consideration later, and to ensure that all issues raised that may delay the project or affect its success are reported, dealt with and traced through to resolution. A lack of awareness and control over problems, particularly in the testing of complex software, can lead to disaster.

All necessary systems and processes must be documented as they are developed. This is never done properly after the event. Process modelling tools, flowcharting and standard templates can be used effectively to reduce the effort required and improve standards. Advantages of good documentation are that it can be used for training purposes later on and makes system maintenance much easier. A central repository of documentation with on-line access to those who need it, makes the control, distribution and currency of systems specifications and other procedural documentation a much more practical proposition than hitherto.

6. Monitor progress

Ongoing monitoring will allow problems to be identified early and resolved before they have an adverse effect on the overall project timetable, quality of the deliverables or cost. This was done through maintaining the project plan up to date and having regular team and steering committee meetings, as appropriate. The need for communication and involving all parties is paramount to success, especially where plans are being changed.

A highly supportive culture is important to ensure staff are comfortable to raise their hand and ask for help when they need it or are not afraid to be the messenger of bad news when things appear to be going badly.

7. Close out

Once a project is completed, the level of success should be measured against the originally defined critical success factors. This success should be celebrated and shared with the whole team.

It is very rare that a project is completed without any outstanding items, or minor quality shortfalls. It is essential to review and deal with them. After a suitable settling in period, perform a post implementation review to ensure the new system works as specified and institute a strategy of ongoing review and continuous improvement.

Project life cycle

For projects involving system development or enhancement, we implemented a formal project life cycle (PLC) methodology. The PLC provided a uniform control environment to govern development, maintenance and enhancement of systems.

The PLC seeks to ensure that systems development is a business driven process with appropriate involvement from all potentially affected parties, there is shared responsibility between user management and technology areas for the success of all projects and the degree of control reflects the risk inherent in the project.

We used a risk assessment methodology during the initial project planning phase in order to ascertain whether the full PLC need be applied, or whether a quick path development process would be more appropriate because the project was relatively low risk. A consistent scoring methodology was developed to measure project criticality. It included numerical judgements in ten areas:

- the project's overall complexity;
- the potential impact on customers;
- the criticality and volatility of the affected business environment;
- technical or hardware risk;
- the systems development environment;
- pressures to meet goals or objectives;
- assets at risk;
- the value and volumes of transactions to be processed;
- the expected quality of business/user participation in the process;
- the legal, regulatory and reporting aspects of the planned system or enhancement.

Each of these factors was scored individually, weighted and an overall score established. Where this score exceeded a predetermined threshold, the use of the full PLC was mandatory. Below this threshold, the project's sponsor decided which approach to adopt.

The PLC clearly establishes roles and responsibilities for systems project development. All projects must have a business sponsor, who appoints a business manager for the project. His responsibilities include identifying and documenting the new system requirements, ensuring full definition of the system functionality, acceptance of delivered applications, user procedures and committing user resources to the project. This all ensures that projects are appropriately business-driven.

In addition, the PLC defines roles and responsibilities for other key groups, such as controllers, database manager, technology and data centre management.

Each project, following the full development cycle, goes through five main phases. These are, first, problem definition and scoping, which includes formal project initiation, terms of reference, risk assessment and a feasibility study. Phase 2 is the functional specification, a detailed review of the problem and the suggested solution. Phase 3 is the design and construction, covering detailed design, programming and system testing. The fourth phase relates to implementation, which includes preparation of the infrastructure, user training, user acceptance and environment testing, conversion and changeover; and finally a post-implementation review. After each phase, a formal sign-off from all key parties is required to ensure the project remains on track and continues to meet the original requirements and specifications.

Programme management

In any large organization, there will be many projects in progress at any one time all vying for scarce resources, and all with differing levels of importance. In addition, there will be interdependencies between projects such that a delay in one will have adverse knock-on effects on others. This brings complexities over and above managing just individual projects separately and therefore a programme management methodology is needed to address these.

Once again, the bank employed a risk-based methodology to highlight those areas of key management concern and where action was needed to stop something going wrong. It was very important that this methodology be seen to be supportive. Projects on schedule continue to be managed by their own project managers through to successful conclusion without interference from senior management. Those projects in risk of failing were investigated to ascertain what needed to be done to bring them back on track, for example by finding and applying additional resources to critical areas.

In order to achieve this, the bank established a centralized database of high-level project data, including project milestones, assumptions made in the planning, issues needing resolution, and interdependencies on areas outside the project manager's control. Each of these items was scored on the basis that, if they went wrong (e.g. a milestone not being achieved on time, an assumption being incorrect), what would be the impact on meeting the overall objectives of the project on time? A second score measured the likelihood of that adverse event happening.

This allowed all projects to be reviewed together and a prioritized list drawn up of the most critical issues of the moment. Management could address these in the correct order of priority. The scores were updated on a regular basis, new issues raised and old issues deleted on a real time basis by the project managers. This allowed senior management at their regular weekly or other routine meetings to review together the most up to date status of all critical projects.

Box 7.5 Managing the merger

The merger of Chemical Bank and Chase Manhattan Bank to form the largest US bank was obviously a mammoth undertaking. Within the UK this meant bringing together and rationalizing over 4,000 staff from the two institutions spread over six separate locations, and integrating extensive business operations in trading, client management, global operating services and private banking.

As far as possible, the merger had to be seen to be an internal event with a minimum of disruption to our customers. Nevertheless, this meant consolidating, for example, dealing rooms with some 600 dealers and the associated operations and support services. It included combining the payment systems of both banks and all accounting, for customer accounts as well as the bank's internal ledgers.

The overall objectives of the merger process were to complete the integration as quickly as possible, maintain or improve standards of customer service, realize operating savings, select the best people and processes from both banks and still maintain control over all business operations. It was recognized that all this had to be accomplished against a background of tremendous staff insecurity, confusion and, in many cases, resistance to change.

A review with senior managers who had been through the previous merger of Chemical Bank with Manufacturers Hanover highlighted the main lessons to be learned from that experience. These related primarily to the people related issues, namely:

- Be aware of and respect cultural differences.
- Expect the unexpected, and get used to ambiguity.
- Communicate, communicate, communicate to help staff morale.
- Do not concentrate only on the merger, to the exclusion of all other activities.
- Maintain operating controls at all times.

Once management appointments had been decided, it was possible to start on the tasks ahead. Within the UK, we established a centralized merger office, reporting directly to the senior country manager, in order to co-ordinate all merger projects. This was staffed by a manager and eight project analysts and given the following objectives:

- Establish consistent project standards and methodologies.
- Manage overall programme risk, interdependencies and change control.
- Ensure full communication of merger status and issues.
- Facilitate and assist project teams.

A merger task force with representatives of all the key functional support and operational areas (e.g. Finance, Technology, Facilities, Operations, Human Resources, Credit) from both banks acted as a steering committee. Expediency was recognized to be more important than perfection, and it was decided to select suites of systems instead of individual applications. This minimized conversion and operating risk and the number of new system interfaces that had to be built.

In order to cover all activities, over sixty merger implementation and project teams were set up, containing representatives from both banks. They were charged with making the merger happen for their respective areas of responsibility. Cognisant of the lessons learned, this process was started at an offsite teambuilding day for about 250 staff with the specific objectives of having full communication, involvement and participation of all critical staff from the earliest opportunity.

Initially, the scene was set through senior management presenting the vision of the new bank in the UK and the overall merger objectives and goals ahead. We emphasized the need for urgency, commitment, accountability and responsibility in everyone and stressed the importance of multi-disciplinary teams working together in order to achieve all the thousands of tasks ahead on time. Future managers were being honed to face the challenges and activities of the coming months.

These presentations were followed by the project teams working together with a facilitator to agree, in particular:

- their overall objectives and strategy;
- what they wanted to carry forward from their old organization;
- committing, individually and together, to get the job done.

While individual teams were empowered to manage their own projects, the programme management methodology of reporting milestones and their achievement to the merger office was employed throughout. The data was made widely available as an on-line database to ensure full communication with everyone involved. In addition, we used the risk assessment based methodology and interview technique widely to support project managers and highlight key issues affecting the merger's overall success and timeliness.

Through the regular meetings of the merger task force, these key issues could be discussed and decisions made quickly at a sufficiently high level. They also established the ownership and accountability for resolving problems and allocated the necessary tasks to the appropriate areas in a highly efficient and timely manner.

The process was supplemented by internal consultants carrying out health checks with project managers on a face-to-face basis through regular supportive interviews. These proved to be very popular with managers as a quick and easy way for them to ensure their voices were heard and their concerns taken seriously and acted upon promptly.

Summary

This chapter has described how Chemical Bank UK managed and reviewed continuously its processes for potential improvement and also how disciplined projects brought about the necessary change to cope with the increasing challenges facing us. The approach balanced not only getting the job done but also integrated dealing with the people issues effectively as an integral part of the whole. It allowed us both to achieve our business goals and our people to perform at their best.

Competition is getting tougher, the pace of change is quicker, the demands are ever more complex. Given the effort that has gone into creating the new merged organization, the work we have put into retraining our people and improving the way things are done, we are looking forward to the future.

CHAPTER EIGHT

Business transformation at MLC

*Oona Nielssen, Global Communications Manager, Lend Lease Property**

This is story about a company, MLC, which when faced with a rapidly changing market, and serious competition, knew it was a case of change or die. Rather than 'rip through the place with a razor', it went to its employees and asked them to lead the transformation. The employees were the focus of the transformation and in turn their willingness and ability to focus on customers and shareholders produced turnaround results.

Another key feature of this case was that MLC's leadership team had the consistency and follow-through to delegate account-ability and provide full support at every step of the way. Under-pinning the mobilisation of employees and committed leadership were a unified management philosophy, constant measurement of progress and – above all – reward for achievements and celebration of success. As a result, MLC has moved in only a few years from being a fuddy-duddy, mainly insurance, company to being a funky funds management company. This case study is about how it happened.

*With contributions from: Jim Baker, Martin Crawford, Marinela Mendes, Clare Moran, Jan Pieters, Clare Ridding, Peter Scott, Geoffrey Summerhayes, Sine Trewartha and Keith Yee.

Superannuation is fairly conservative, fairly intense, but MLC have tried to take that and make it a fun place to work for people and give them lots of opportunities and lots of skills and training to go where they want.

Claire Ridding, Service Culture Manager

What is MLC?

MLC is the financial services arm of Lend Lease – an Australian based global property and funds management company. MLC was formerly named The Mutual Life & Citizens Assurance Company Limited. Founded as a traditional life insurance company over 100 years ago, MLC has become a major manager of modern, unit-linked investment products. The company now provides superannuation, savings and investment services, plus renewable protection products to individuals, trustees and businesses. It has 1.5 million customers, out of a total Australian population of 18 million people.

The market

The Australian investment market has been changing rapidly. The government has shifted the responsibility for retirement funding to individuals through tax incentives and legislation. They have mandated that 7% of everybody's base salary must be invested in superannuation. This will increase shortly to 10%.

The demographic changes mean that the 'baby boomer bubble' will not be supportable through traditional government-funded age pension schemes. In the wealthy, welfare state that was Australia in the post-war years, people expected to work all their lives, buy a house and retire with a reasonable government pension until they died. The population growth has slowed and the proportion of people dependent on welfare is large compared with the proportion of people who contribute to government revenue.

There is now a heightened awareness of investment. Australia has changed from a country where most people invest their entire wealth in the family home, to a country where mixed investment portfolios are common. The provision of financial advice is now accepted as something applicable to everyone. For example the proportion of the population owning shares has increased from 15% to 40% in just 5 years.

MLC's transformation

Lend Lease bought MLC in 1985, when the company was already 100 years old. Then in 1996 under the leadership of CEO, David Clarke, a transformation process was introduced. The seeds for the change were sown in late 1993 with the formation of the Simplification Team. The aim now was to change rapidly from a hierarchical, convention bound company to one which achieves world best practice standards for financial institutions. For MLC, a cost reduction of 40% was seen as necessary for survival and longevity.

Transformation triggers: Marketplace, shareholders, people

There were three main triggers for transformation. One was the marketplace. The combination of deregulation of the banking industry and new government measures to enforce personal retirement saving means that competition is fierce. MLC used to sell contractual premiums, where people locked into an agreement to pay premiums for 10, 20 or 30 years. Under that regime profit was 'locked in' at the time of sale and the penalties for early withdrawal meant customer loyalty was guaranteed.

As customers become financially aware and more active in making investments they start to question the value of both existing and potential investments. As a result, customer retention is based on a combination of the investment performance of funds and of the service provided. In MLC's case, both investment performance and service needed improving. Australian consumers were demanding less complexity and were angry about the commission payments to agents, which were often not disclosed on printed material.

Another trigger was the aggressive owner – Lend Lease – and its 33,000 shareholders. Lend Lease has had a steady growth in profit every year for the last 20 years. It has continued to expand into Asia, Europe and North and South America. Lend Lease demands that the businesses it holds be the best in their respective fields. MLC, as the financial services arm, had been a significant contributor to this profit and needed to ensure it could continue to meet shareholder expectations.

The third trigger was the people. To respond to market demands for service and investment returns, MLC needed to effect radical changes in the way people worked. It also needed to create a dynamic and rewarding environment to attract and retain the people it required to support its vision. Lend Lease is also very much a people focused company, with very progressive employee policies. For MLC there was no question of not focusing on people during a transformation effort.

How MLC does business

All products are sold through a network of financial advisers. They are retailed through both MLC advisers and independents. 90% of new business comes through financial advisers so the retail effort is predominantly focused on this distribution channel.

Most transactions occur over the phone. Today, 10,000 calls per day are received by MLC's three call centres in Sydney, Melbourne and Brisbane. There are an additional 5,000 mail initiated requests per day. Five years ago there were about 2,000 phone calls and the same number of mail requests per day. The figures reflect that a significant focus for the transformation effort was around the work of front line staff in the call centres.

The transformation process

The transformation process had three steps:

1. Simplify and reduce the number of products;

2. Simplify administrative processes and;

3. Initiate a cultural change that would bring those processes to life. MLC found very early on that you can change processes but the only way to bring the processes to life is through the attitudes of people.

These activities were managed by a core team, consisting of senior project managers and external consultants. At regular intervals, progress was reviewed by the senior management team using a steering forum known as the Project Control Group (PCG). The PCG concept was taken directly from Lend Lease where it is used in construction projects. This is quite novel within financial services and is a good example of synergy of management practices between the two parts of the group.

Product simplification

Product simplification was necessary because there were 108 years of history and therefore 108 years of product development without rationalisation. Before improving processes, the products had to be simplified. The aim was to bring all products into a simple transparent form, with a common look and feel, a common fee structure, high service standards, readily understood statements and a good range of investment choices.

In the product simplification exercise, MLC's actively sold product range was reduced from 35 products to just 13 core products. As an example, the 3 core traditional insurance products used to have about 340 different variations resulting in very complex systems requirements. The simplification exercise reduced the number of variations to just 22. The superannuation area had 10 products which it reduced to only 3.

A set of guiding principles for simplification was developed:

- Be customer not product focused

- Provide products and services that represent value for money

- Maintain lowest cost provider strategy

- Focus on market segments which are profitable and in which we have a sustainable competitive advantage

- Adhere to the spirit and not just the wording of regulations

- Behave in an ethical manner at all times

- Use only simple language – avoid jargon.

Teams were selected to examine the products, review the commission structure and develop plans for future service delivery. These teams were cross-functional and their members were selected for their experience and attitude.

The simplification was done by taking a 'snapshot' of every product and assessing it against the guiding principles. Each product was also analysed for sales and profitability, projected future sales and areas of overlap. For each product the teams then prepared a rationale for keeping it, changing it or throwing it out.

Customers on old products were traded up. That is they were offered the benefits of new products which do not require contractual contributions and do not attract high fees when contributions are increased. As the number of superannuation products reduced from 10 to 3, about 170,000 superannuation customers were traded up.

One of the groups most affected by this change to products was the distribution network – the advisers. In 1990 MLC had 1,500 tied advisers and today there are only 600. Advisers were critical to introducing new products as their commission was now based on an ongoing relationship with the client, rather than an up front payment for the sale of the product with little reward for ongoing service.

Funds under management have continued to increase. The market for investment funds is competitive and full of choice so it is only through providing consistent returns and top service that the business grows. Product simplification aimed to provide choice without complication. The continued growth in market share indicates the success of this.

Process simplification

Process simplification was the banner initiative of the transformation. Several tools were employed under this banner, each selected to fit the workplace.

Innovate

Innovate is a tool aimed at surfacing individual initiatives. It is essentially a competition where cash is paid for ideas based on their merit to the business. This is done by providing an ideas forum where people describe the idea, how it adds value, what resources are required and how they would implement it. People are then asked to implement their ideas and each implemented idea is also rewarded with cash.

Each month winning ideas are paid cash and everybody who submits an idea gets a windmill they can stick on their computer.

When this program was run, pretty soon peer pressure meant everyone wanted a windmill and some people had more than one. It was a self-perpetuating ideas mill.

Breakthrough

99% of people who come to work every day want to do a good job and the only things that get in the way are dumb processes, inadequate training or skilling and inadequate systems or technology. When they feel that the environment is being created for them to do extraordinary things it is a snowball that you can't stop.

Peter Scott, Chief Operating Officer

The breakthrough process was adapted from a book by Robert Schaffer.[1] The underlying philosophy is to release latent potential in the organization by providing the encouragement and resources required to deliver real results quickly. The approach enables front line staff to set and achieve clear, compelling and demonstrable improvement goals in a short but manageable timeframe. At MLC selected groups of up to eight people concentrated their efforts on solving problems within a time limit of eight weeks. The breakthrough process is highly structured and quite rigorous. It goes like this:

1. Nominate people for teams on the basis that they are pro-active and think they have an idea to try.

2. Form them into a team and induct them into the breakthrough process.

3. The team brainstorms an idea to work on. The idea must be conceived, measured and implemented within eight weeks

4. The team maps the process they are seeking to improve.

5. They brainstorm the process and then work out what to remove or change.

6. The team gets access to information about costing, timing, etc, and any training required.

7. Measurements, goals and milestones are set and reported on throughout the eight week period.

8. The project is finalised and the team rewarded.

People participating in these projects can request leave from regular duties for specific tasks, but are not usually full time on breakthrough.

The impact for each of the breakthrough teams has to be measurable – ideally a cost impact but also a service impact. The teams are charged with being quite commercial about the accountability process. The implementation of these ideas has so far reduced about $7m from MLC's cost base.

Some examples of breakthrough projects include:

To reduce the time it takes to check signatures when withdrawing money from a unit trust by 75% in eight weeks. The team had to clean up the filing room where all the signatures were kept by reorganising the filing system. By measuring the time taken to check signatures before and after the reorganisation, the 75% target was proven to have been reached, and a saving on labour costs of $100,000 per annum was achieved.

To reduce the time it takes to process an address change in the superannuation maintenance team from five days to the same day. The team changed the process so that MLC stopped requesting customers put change of address notification in writing – notification over the phone was fine. There were no immediate cost savings because of a security check confirming the change was put in place, but there was a huge improvement in customer service.

> Some of the small projects are the most exciting projects because of the type of people who are doing it. A young receptionist who did a cost benefit analysis for upgrading the fax machine, for example, saved $10,000 per year.
>
> Jan Pieters, Project Manager

Obviously not all projects would work using the breakthrough format. While it is ideal for processes without too many dependencies, some things such as IT projects were too big to fit the criteria.

Core process redesign

Core process redesign (CPR) is a tool for larger departments and processes. With people having participated in breakthrough projects, their minds were attuned to the discipline of change and were able to tackle longer processes. CPR can involve quite large processes and take up to six months. Typically things such as customer communications issues, distribution issues, IT or regulatory processes would be addressed using CPR.

CPR has three criteria. It has to improve service, lower costs and improve careers for employees. If a project doesn't fit those criteria, then it does not go ahead.

Departments such as finance and marketing which are less process oriented took a slightly different approach. They examined each activity and assessed the value it was adding to employees, customers and shareholders. Every activity was assessed and decisions were made to remove, enhance or change that activity after assessment.

One large process that was redesigned was the flow of work between the call centres and the administration function. These were brought together as one group. Every process needed to be integrated. This stopped the artificial separation between the receipt of customer requests in the call centres and their subsequent processing in the administration function. A major cultural benefit was that CPR helped eliminate the inherent buck-passing of responsibility for completion that had existed previously.

Cultural change

This was an approach rather than a process. People and their attitudes were recognised very early on as being the only important element in achieving a transformation. The people issues were embedded in all the change efforts. In particular the REACH and people development initiatives illustrate this.

REACH

REACH is an acronym for resolution, empathy, accuracy, convenience and honesty. It is the tool to embed the cultural and behavioural changes required for the transformation effort. Put simply REACH is based on values, for which employees identified specific behaviours they would deliver in their workplace. So rather than being an imposed value statement, it was brought to life by work teams agreeing on what behaviours represented those values. REACH was implemented in parallel with process simplification.

People development

The acquisition of new skills can be the largest investment in a transformation process. At MLC this was achieved through local skills coordinators, through a people development team and through giving people the information, support and resources they required to make changes happen.

People were thrown into challenging leadership positions. On teams they were asked to come up with solutions themselves. People were handpicked for their attitudes and the learning followed. Rather than have a structured skill development programme throughout MLC, there was an action learning process. The combination of focused time scales and delegated responsibility and authority created the perfect learning environment. Learning was sought out as and when it was needed, with the company supporting the individuals' efforts.

People were enormously motivated because they worked on their own idea and not somebody else's. The incentive to continue and complete was very high. Learning outcomes were often achieved through networking, delegation, and project management because the implementation of a lot of the projects had to be negotiated with other stakeholders.

> We underestimated the power of the people and their ability to innovate and contribute. It was rewarding to watch people grow and grow beyond our wildest expectations.
>
> **Geoffrey Summerhayes, General Manager, Customer Service**

Additionally the 'towards leadership' initiative was launched. This was a formal leadership programme in which senior people worked with external providers to cofacilitate key activities and events. This created an effective network of mentors throughout the company, increasing the skills of those who participated in the programme and those who were mentors and facilitators.

Celebration and reward

Significant effort was directed toward acknowledging success and sharing the progress. This was done through incentives such as cash, shares and prizes; through public acknowledgement such as parties, certificates and promotions; and through skills acquisition, career development and provision of new opportunities.

The most outstanding examples of celebration were the 'Breakthrough Expos'. These were mini-fairs held over several hours and attended by nearly everybody in the company. Breakthrough teams set up interactive exhibits to explain and describe their projects. Projects were described with wit, energy and imagination. The expos brought the achievements to life, and showcased the journey in a way no boring report could. Team members got immediate approval from colleagues and managers, all in a party atmosphere.

What happened – the cultural impact

The funny thing is now there seems to be more passion in the people than there is a clear strategy. People are marching in tune but it is not the tune we initially thought it was going to be.
Marinela Mendes, Communications Manager, Product Simplification

As changes began to be implemented, an upward surge in company morale was clear. People felt very empowered. The process worked from the bottom up and was supported from the top down. All the ideas came from employees and all the support came from senior management. The General Managers facilitated cross-functional teams with frontline employees – jumping over middle management. This high level support of day to day operations was very empowering. Additionally people were given facilitation and team leadership skills so that they could take teams through the process.

The common language and the ability to see ideas come to fruition has embedded itself in the MLC culture. Transformation has moved from being a special project, or series of projects, to being business as usual. The business has made transformation a core capability. People are happier. They run the business, they influence the business and the customers know this.

Staff reductions

Losing staff was never an aim of the transformation. However, if processes are simplified it is inevitable that fewer hands will be required. Most reductions were achieved through natural attrition and self-selection. There is a young work force so staff turnover is inevitable. When a large downsizing in a department became apparent, any natural turnover was replaced with temporary employees.

Across the company there were only limited retrenchments throughout the turnaround – which is significantly different from many traditional business process re-engineering efforts. The entire process resulted in approximately 240 fewer jobs and 1,000 fewer advisers. At the same time an Enterprise Development Agreement (EDA) was struck between the Financial Services Union and MLC. This agreement set a benchmark for workplace agreements in the Australian financial industry.

The results of transformation

In the period from December 1995 to December 1997, MLC achieved the following returns on its investment in transformation:

- Funds under management grew from $20.4b to $25.4b – an increase of 25%

- Staff numbers decreased by 18% from 1,377 full time equivalents to 1,135

- A corresponding 51% productivity increase on funds under management – rising from $14.8m to $22.4m per employee

- The ratio of non-sales related expenses to funds under management dropped by 40% from 1.42% to 0.85%

- Costs are forecast to drop by 19% from $266m for year-ending June 1996, to $215m for year-ending June 1998.

Conclusion

This transformation successfully integrated cultural, attitudinal and structural issues. It was led from the top, but driven from the bottom. The outcome is an energised, skilled and motivated work force who really understand how it feels to be empowered. The focus on the people in the business and their abilities, means that customer service is brought to life for the customers and the financial adviser network. The shareholders were the beneficiaries of the transformation, with the financial results speaking for themselves.

MLC has embedded the learning from these changes into the business. People are better able to make things happen and to take responsibility. The changes continue. The head office in Sydney is currently undergoing a renovation where team spaces are being created. The physical environment is being constructed to reflect the culture desired and to enhance productivity and communication.

As a result of its transformation process and the successful integration of many of the practices into business as usual, MLC is now a world class competitor in funds management, comparing very favourably with world's best practice for the industry.

Reference

1. Schaffer, Robert H. (1990) 'The Breakthrough Strategy: Using Short term Success to build the High Performance Organisation', Harper Collins

CHAPTER NINE

Using modern technology to build new capabilities

Clive Holtham, Bull Information Systems Professor of Information Management, City University Business School

Introduction

There is no questioning the operational significance of information technology within modern financial services. Nor can there be any doubt of the potential of IT for developing not just new business opportunities, but also entirely new market-places. What is being constantly questioned, however, is whether IT actually provides value for money, and whether it is successfully contributing to the wider strategic objectives of the business. The innovative dimension of IT also poses a challenge or threat, particularly to existing and well-established financial institutions. They face a particular need to re-engineer existing business processes, if they are to compete with 'greenfield' competitors who may be able to exploit new technologies more rapidly.

Frameworks

Information technology plays a fundamental role in building and rebuilding financial services businesses, and in new product development. The aim of this chapter is to examine the strategic role of information technology in the process of change. Its particular perspective is to argue that it is *not* the purchase or application of information technology *per se* which brings competitive advantage. It is rather the way that technology is skilfully combined with actions and decisions in other key domains.

As Peter Keen (1991, pp. 51–52) has pointed out:

> information technology is just one element albeit often a strong one, in competitive positioning. It cannot compensate for fundamental weaknesses in market strategy, cost structure, and organization. This is illustrated by the case of Merrill Lynch's Cash Management Account, a dramatic IT innovation that enabled the company to build a new customer base of a million affluent individuals but did not keep it from drifting badly in the following decade because of failure to manage its cost base.

There have been several general models and frameworks to illustrate the different roles that information technology can play in organizational change. It is worth reviewing a number of these here.

A long-standing model (Figure 9.1) is that of McFarlan *et al.* (1982). This model suggests that firms seeking to derive business opportunities through IT should look at their position on a grid involving two dimensions: the strategic impact of their existing IT application, and the strategic impact of their future IT application choices. The four quadrants of this grid are seen to reflect four types of IT environments, namely:

- *Strategic*, where firms are on the one hand dependent on current IT activities, and on the other hand, have IT applications under development that are crucial to their future competitive positioning, and business success.

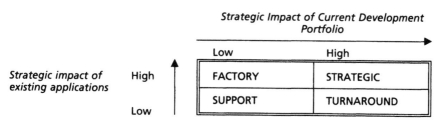

Fig. 9.1 Assessing the role of IT in organizational change.

● *Turnaround*, where current IT activities although they may be seen to furnish IT support, are not crucial to business performance, but future IT applications are in essence strategic and highly important to the firm.

● *Factory*, where the firm is dependent on IT support for current activities, and where development choices necessitate continuous updating which are not dependent on the firm's ability to compete.

● *Support*, where IT activities and applications under development are neither critical to existing operations, or vital for strategic success.

Much of financial services' use of IT up to the early 1990s fell into the factory or support quadrants. Much of the subsequent investment in IT has the aim of moving into the turnaround quadrant, poised then to move into strategic.

Another fundamental categorization was made by Shoshana Zuboff (1988), who contrasted informating with automating.

More recently, a model that prefigured the whole business process re-engineering movement was developed by Venkatraman (1990), as part of the MIT Management in the 90s study (Scott Morton, 1990). This model developed Zuboff's distinction into a five-layer model (Figure 9.2), where the lowest two layers were seen as evolutionary, the top three being revolutionary. Venkatraman concluded that the vast bulk of computerization has been focused at levels one and two, with very little indeed being at the higher levels. Subsequent expe-

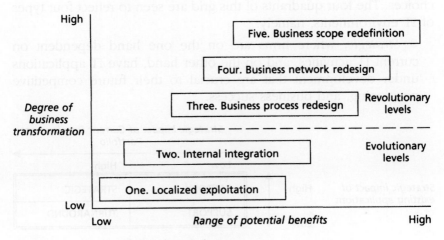

Fig. 9.2 Five levels of IT-induced change.

riences even up to the time of writing have tended to confirm that businesses find it much easier to evolve than to be revolutionary in their application of information technology.

The 'Barriers model' has been developed at City University Business School. As can be seen from its physical layout (Figure 9.3), it symbolizes that there is very little possibility of any direct link between information technology and business success. This is because the way that most businesses work, even if there was a technology with near-direct potential, it would still have to overcome a series of barriers to be deployed to strategic advantage. In reality, almost all technology innovations have to surmount such barriers, and many fail to do so.

The barriers are shown in a hierarchy. It needs first to be emphasized that it is rarely technology in itself that brings the advantage. The advantage as Zuboff suggests, is the way that technology reconfigures information. Information is therefore shown as the element directly closest to strategy. But before that, two other barriers need to be overcome. The first is the nature of the organization, which may resist or be unable to take on board the changes or improvements on offer. The second is the need to build, out of a variety of technological components, the integrated systems that will actually deliver the improved information.

Running throughout this hierarchy of barriers are two further ones. *People* are critical, both in relation to their overall attitudes to technology and change, perhaps encapsulated in the idea of organi-

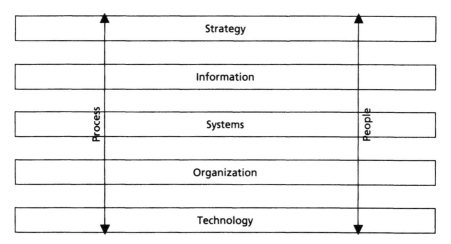

Fig. 9.3 The barriers to organizational change (Source: City University, London).

zational culture, as well as a result of their immediate skills in managing and using IT. The idea of *process*, in contrast to the formal organizational structure, has received considerable emphasis as a barrier as a result of the substantial body of work on BPR.

There are relatively few organizations, including in financial services, that can be said to have found a consistent way of removing or even reducing the barriers to the full exploitation of information technology.

Technology architecture

There are many different ways of analysing the development of modern business computing and information technology. Figure 9.4 presents a particular illustration of that history.

It should be noted here that all three of the eras have equal validity. It is common to hear the phrase 'legacy' system used to describe those developed in the 1980s and 1970s, typically using proprietary mainframe and minicomputer technologies. It may well be that the mainframe is now considerably less appropriate and economic than it was twenty years ago. Much data processing can be carried out on non-mainframe machines, and the bulk of expenditure on IT in financial services is now on PCs and networks, rather than mainframes. But the importance of central standardized databases remains of fundamental significance in financial services, regardless of what type of technology they are stored on.

If mainframes are 'legacy' machines, then so too are the vast bulk of PCs, which in many financial services organizations are only 'loosely connected' through their respective local and wide area networks. Typical uses of such networks will be for low-level

Era	Characteristics	Revolutionary feature
Stage 1. Mainframe	Single unified data standard	Central, shared databases
Stage 2. PC	Personal processing and flexibility	Individual empowerment
Stage 3. Group	Sharing of soft data and expertise	Group collaboration

Fig. 9.4 The development of modern business computing.

functions such as printer-sharing, E-mail and mainframe terminal emulation. Such PCs run the risk of becoming legacies. This is because they have over-emphasized an individualistic model of business computing. Such a model is highly appropriate to isolated individuals, such as home users, authors and perhaps university students, but far less appropriate for corporate organizations of any degree of complexity.

The reaction against the PC can take an essentially evolutionary route, with the idea of converting the PC into the centrepiece of an environment for sharing information and knowledge. Or it can take a revolutionary form, with the argument that what is needed for most business purposes is a diskless colour terminal, no longer subject to high cost maintenance and support activities. Such a terminal has been dubbed the 'network computer' (NC).

Managing legacy systems

The first half of the 1990s saw radical changes in the organization and sourcing of the IT of many large corporations, including some financial institutions. Common topics in this context were:

- the reduction in size or elimination of central IT departments;
- the general move away from centralized processing;
- the outsourcing of the IT function itself to contractors.

Roche (1992) reviewed the evolution of IT in Manufacturers Hanover Bank from 1980 to 1991. He found that the 1980s was oriented to branch office automation, reducing the size of the branch network, and aggressive cost-cutting. To promote innovation, in 1986 it set up a high-powered group of internal consultants called Strategic Technology and Research (STAR).

This group was preoccupied with addressing strategic problems such as foreign exchange risk analysis, and the difficult planning processes including multiple products. 'However, one of its most significant ideas was to work at completely re-engineering the corporation as a whole from an information technology point of view.'

This had a major impact on IT itself though, with a proposal to reduce the five major US data centres to two, which later became one, with the attention subsequently turned to global consolidation. This was a complete reversal from the previous fifteen years, which had seen a strong thrust to decentralization.

There was absolutely no question of downsizing from mainframes in a firm with global 24-hour-per-day communications and very heavy volumes of transaction processing. The proliferation of personal computers and other distributed processing systems had continued to raise concerns within the bank over security . . . the growing demands of its worldwide customers called for greater *global* control over its many services that were being extended.

Identifying the technology's potential

A major benefit of information technology comes from the way that it enables information to be reconfigured. A good summary of examples of this reconfiguration can be found in Davenport (1993), summarized in Table 9.1.

At this stage only a few observations need to be made on this list. Much remains to be done in several of the areas. In the Analytical area, Cheng Ann Khoo (1989) found significant weaknesses in the management information available within the banking environment. He classified analytical information into five main types: financial, performance measurement, risk-related, regulatory and strategic. Since his study was completed, a number of graphical examples of information failure in financial services have underlined the validity of his conclusion.

The penultimate item in Figure 9.5 – intellectual – is already the subject of some sustained innovation in financial services. In Sweden

Table 9.1 How IT enables information to be reconfigured

Impact	Explanation
Automational	Eliminating human labour
Informational	Capturing process information for understanding
Sequential	Changing process sequence, including parallelism
Tracking	Monitoring process status/objects
Analytical	Improving analysis of information; decision making
Geographical	Co-ordinating across distances
Integrative	Co-ordination of tasks and processes
Intellectual	Capture and distribute intellectual assets
Disintermediating	Eliminating intermediaries

and world-wide, Skandia has become preoccupied with the notion of its competitive advantage lying in its ability to create and accelerate the circulation of its intellectual capital. The company has produced a supplementary annual report focusing on its intellectual as opposed to its financial capital. And management have created a position of Vice President of Intellectual Capital.

It is perfectly feasible to produce a roll call of the technologies that will or may underpin such reconfiguration of information. Any such list would include the following:

- voice processing;
- multimedia, video conferencing;
- smart card;
- client server;
- executive information systems;
- workflow;
- groupware;
- document image processing;
- internet;
- unmanned branches;
- expert systems;
- EDI;
- EFTPOS;
- electronic cash.

However, although the physical information technologies are of key importance, which particular technology is of value at any given time is very much a movable feast. All large financial institutions will be at least experimenting with almost every item on the above list, but that does not mean that all such experiments will eventually become commercially viable.

Moving from product-based to customer-based systems

It is possible to describe most financial institutions that developed from their nineteenth century roots as 'producer-centric'. Now this is not entirely fair, as several major organizations developed out of co-operative or mutual roots. But even those organizations that remain mutual by ownership, can still operate in a producer-centric fashion. This phenomenon is not limited to financial services – it applies to much of the public sector also.

If some of the theorists of future organizational forms are to be believed, then there is a need to move to a perspective that is 'customer-centric'. Often such a view is interpreted too narrowly. For example, a decade ago it was common for banks to create an 'integrated' customer database. This was clearly of importance for providing e.g. branch managers with an overall perspective of the customer. At great expense, databases were then amended or updated to permit integration.

As time moved on, two issues began to emerge:

● Different business units needed to respond to the speed of change in their market-place.

● Banks were often eliminating their branch administration, in favour of more efficient regional centres. This process was facilitated by the integrated databases. But the management systems and procedures put in place then reduced customer service. For example ineffective recording of customer telephone enquiries (a 'soft' system) meant that some of the personal contact, admittedly expensive, in the old system, was eliminated.

The integrated databases had tended to integrate only the hard/formal/structured system. They had not re-engineered the end-to-end business process. They had actually reinforced some of the weaknesses inherent in the producer-centred approach.

A consumer-centric approach would start from a number of assumptions absent from the producer-centric approach:

● twenty-four hours a day, seven days a week, full service availability;

● fast response to enquiries or service requests;

● in the great majority of cases, resolution of the request/inquiry at the first attempt.

Such approaches were distinct features of new operations such as First Direct or Direct Line. They are also symbolized in the introduction of multimedia kiosks. In work carried out in the UK, Thomas Cook have placed travel kiosks in branches of Natwest Bank, and vice versa. In Barcelona, under Project Vereda, public sector service-providers have collaborated with local banks to produce a public kiosk that also enables banking and insurance transactions to take place.

Direct marketing is an area that has seen considerable growth as a result of a desire to convert the raw data held in name and address files into usable customer information. There is increasingly sophisticated analysis based on the address/postcode matched to socio-economic characteristics.

It is also possible to draw on internally generated data to create individualized mailshots. Winger and Edelman (1990) illustrate how Merrill Lynch developed a new investment product, which they introduced to customers by mailing a personalized portfolio analysis that showed what the return would be with an investment in that new product.

One of the problems in moving to customer-centric operations has been that the first forty years of business computing has been dominated by the processing of data, mostly 'hard'. It has been essentially a data age, rather than an information age.

Many of the key areas of relationship in any service industry are 'soft', driven by specific interests and issues for the customer, rather than by narrow data processing needs. So what is necessary is the capability to capture and share the softer data. Banks are beginning to explore such approaches, perhaps in specific areas such as very high value customers, corporate finance or marketing intelligence systems.

The major constraints on moving to a synergistic linkage of hard and soft data no longer relate to information technology.. The technology needed is already here, and it is sure to become increasingly economic. The major problem is understanding how the needs of customer service can be reinterpreted in an era where soft data – ideas, opinions, views – can be processed and shared as easily as basic numeric and text data. This is a task for managers not technologists, but there has been a communications failure – technologies are not interpreted enough in business terms.

We have found that the understandable conservatism to exchange and share is being broken down in some places. There are now organizations (usually quite small ones) where every single customer contact is logged, enabling a full profile of that customer to be shared across time, across space and across hierarchical levels. This is the beginning of information-age thinking and practice and a move away from factory-type thinking.

Some larger organizations outside banking have opted for this approach; it remains to be seen whether an innovator could deploy new technologies in this field to improve dramatically customer service in banking.

Reversing traditional management fears and concerns over IT

One IT line manager in a bank interviewed by Dockery (1990) noted that:

> The strategic use of IT must come from the business unit managers – it must be business driven. The IT division can only make them aware of emerging technology, and technologies. We can suggest to them the new usage and the ways of doing things, and they feel quite comfortable with that, but still there is the need for them to be more involved in the process.

A number of strategies have been adopted in financial services to create a climate where greater involvement can be achieved. One increasingly common method is to transfer some or all of the responsibility for the management of IT from the central computer department towards the business unit.

A major study carried out by the West London Training and Enterprise Council in 1993 demonstrated that there are still very major shortcomings in the IT skills and awareness of business executives and users at all levels within business units. A minority of organizations have set up major training and awareness campaigns aimed at improving their managers' awareness of IT.

Probably the most significant and most sustained such programme is the CATALYST programme created by British Airways. However, even in this case, great emphasis is placed on the way that IT skills are being developed, not in isolation, but as an integral part of the wider business and human resource development strategy.

A newer problem arising is that of some business managers becoming technology champions, when in fact their perspective should be business-driven.

Building new IT capabilities

One organization that carried out a detailed review of the benefits of building new IT-based capability was Citicorp's Real Estate Group. This is the group concerned with delivering loans to large corporate customers for office buildings. According to Tapscott and Caston (1993):

An initial examination of the group shows weak financial performance, a slow cumbersome process of doing business, and vast portions of time spent by group members in what they considered to be unproductive activities.

Two years after the system implementation and business process redesign, profit center earnings more than doubled. The amount of time to process loans (all in millions of dollars) was reduced by almost 50 per cent. Executive management time spent on 'administrative activities' dropped from 70 to 25 per cent of the day. The number of customers managed per account executive rose by 170 per cent, while the percentage of account executives exceeding their targets increased from less than 6 to 75 per cent. These and other improvements resulted in striking increases in business revenues. at the same time the bank was able to contain its operating costs.

. . . One of the most significant changes was in the nature of the business team itself. In addition to business processes and procedures, the jobs of all corporate Real Estate Personnel were redesigned . . . reflecting their new responsibilities, they became customer service representatives with a focus on the customer rather than internal administration . . . The Corporate Real Estate organization had built a high-performance business team.

The introduction of any technology is in itself a form of change. But as the automating versus informating discussion showed, change is not necessarily beneficial in itself. This has augmented the case for business process redesign as a form of planned, radical change.

Maglitta (1995) described Independence One's success in reducing loan turnaround time by 80 per cent and Nagel and Dove (1991) highlighted the benefits that can accrue from radical review of business processes:

Citicorp Mortgage reduced the time for processing a loan from the industry average of 30 to 60 days, down to 15 days or less, and then to as quick as 15 minutes in some cases.

Some of the changes introduced in the name of BPR basically involve introducing manufacturing techniques to service industries. Banking will never be a manufacturing industry. After health and education it is one of the most deeply personal service industries. So those who are confident that modern technology has the potential to transform banks need to be the first to challenge the introduction of inappropriate manufacturing techniques. It is especially ironic that such techniques are themselves increasingly falling out of favour in factories.

Changing the rules of the game through IT

Three areas are used here to illustrate how information technology can alter some of the basic parameters of a financial services market-place. The first area relates to a fundamental issue – the replacement of cash in the forms of coins and notes, with electronic cash. The second touches on the exploitation of new delivery channels, particularly the Internet. The third is the example of the use of information technology as a mechanism for smaller banks to achieve high levels of international collaboration.

Electronic cash

There are at the time of writing a number of competing products in the field of electronic cash. The major credit card companies are all working on secure credit card transactions over the Internet, but due to the cost structure of credit cards, these are only likely to be useful for a minority of electronic transactions. Two other approaches are more specifically geared to smaller transactions, and to Internet commerce as a whole.

The first is a UK-originated approach – Mondex International. Mondex involves the storage of value on an electronic purse – a smart card. Retailers need to be equipped with Mondex card-readers. Mondex was set up by Natwest, HSBC and BT. The BT link means that the telecom operator is upgrading its payphones so that they are Mondex compatible. This means that any such payphone can be used to download value from a bank account onto a card. Such phones are being located in supermarkets and pubs, for example.

Telephones can also be used to upload value. For example, a taxi driver receiving payment in onto a corporate Mondex card, can pay that in every hour or two via a Mondex public telephone. The significance of the Mondex approach is not simply the potential replacement of notes and coins. It is the conversion of any suitable public telephone into an ATM. Mondex-enabled domestic tel-ephones enable cash transfer directly between two individuals from one card to the other card. The same would be true of Internet transactions, using a Mondex-enabled modem.

An alternative approach to electronic cash is to rely on software to protect the creation, storage and transfer of value. The critical technology here is the encryption software used. A Dutch-based company Digicash NV has been amongst the world leaders in developing such software. Its system is called e-cash, and was piloted for some time, providing its customers with a mythical currency called 'cyber-bucks', which could nonetheless be used to buy a small number of real products.

New delivery channels

An increasing number of banks and insurance companies offer computer banking services through private networks or on-line services. Visa International has introduced home-banking software that allows bank customers to balance chequebooks, pay bills and transfer money between accounts. Meanwhile, Visa Interactive is developing other ways to offer home banking, including a screen-phone, and is working with Worlds Inc. to develop 3-D home banking software.

Some institutions also have established World Wide Web 'home pages', but these often only provide information about their conventional financial services.

> Two of America's leading super-regional bank holding companies, Wachovia Corp. of Winston-Salem, NC and Huntington Bancshares of Columbus, Ohio, have agreed to invest in a savings bank planning to open its doors to the Internet.
>
> The bank, to be known as Security First Network Bank, will operate from a single office in Pineville, Kentucky. Through the acquisition of a computer security firm WebTech, Security First expects to sell to other financial services organizations the technology necessary for their customers to bank on the Internet, including a full range of depositor banking services.

A case of international collaboration

In many sectors of industry, mergers and acquisitions have been a very common method of augmenting the range and reach of a business. But information technology in particular opens up other methods of achieving some of this augmentation. A good example is where the Royal Bank of Scotland and Banco Santander in Spain needed a low-cost, fast electronic payments system to help exporters and others and matching the facilities available to the large multi-national corporations.

The IBOS (inter-bank on-line system) was created in 1991 to

support their reciprocal banking agreements. The requirement for reciprocal services between the two founding banks was identified as generic – likely to be needed by a wide range of other banks. The underlying principles and requirements were defined as:

- *low-cost* – eliminate expensive manual intervention during the funds transfer;

- *high-speed* – reduce the delivery time from days to seconds;

- global – enable banks to operate in other countries without a physical presence;

- common platform – ensure IBOS facilities would be accepted internationally for bank-to-bank and bank-to-customer financial transfers.

This was technically achieved through the definition of a set of core transactions for money transfers, account information and internal bank services.

The messages are transmitted between banks over a global network on a point-to-point basis with no centralized processing or switching hub, using software which allows banks quickly to interface IBOS with their own internal systems. Commercially, the solution involved the creation of IBOS Ltd as an independent entity and the establishment of the IBOS Association of Banks to encourage collaboration and reciprocity.

IBOS is being used by banks from Belgium, Denmark, France, Italy, the Netherlands, Portugal, Spain, the UK and the US. This gives coverage of up to 5,500 branches to service customers' cross-border business. Each new addition strengthens the ability of the entire community to offer reciprocal banking services. IBOS is being employed as a core element in such advanced concepts as fully-electronic 'virtual banking'.

Leveraging the newly developed capabilities

Dockery (1990) noted the significance placed on flexibility and responsiveness by managers in banks:

> Where the business is concerned, one needs to devise an architecture which enables that response to new opportunities, and it has to be an objective of that architecture to facilitate a rapid response to initiatives.

It is very hard to get competitive advantage through just installing a bit of hardware. The only way that you can get competitive advantage is to make your system balanced enough and open enough so that you can react very quickly to market needs.

To this end we can expect to see even more greatly increased emphasis on methodologies that support rapid applications development (RAD), and which enable flexible design and redesign of systems. There is still a great deal of improvement possible through participative systems design. The US Army made dramatic reductions in the time taken to get sign-off to new computer systems, through creating a computer-supported meeting environment which enabled anonymous brainstorming and voting. Supported by facilitators, such approaches begin to offer the prospect of improved productivity in specific areas of executive work.

The centre of gravity in the next decade is likely to shift further away from the 'traditional' IT worker, with a professional background and training in information technology, concerned either with the development of new systems or the day-to-day operation of those systems once developed.

The development of new technologies, particularly those based on advanced telecommunications and object-oriented methods, requires a different and broader range of skills than those encompassed by 'traditional' IT. Also most of the core systems needed have already been physically developed, so some of the prestige and budgets that accrued to large-scale developments will move elsewhere.

It is now being suggested that what is needed to exploit the outputs of new technology is a 'new information professional' (NIP) (Best, 1996), as distinct from the information technology professional. The new information professional will much more typically come from a business background than from an information technology background. Some will be concerned at the operational level with day-to-day information resource management. Other will be engaged in a more strategic exercise to chart the information architecture of the organization, and to ensure that all the systems and processes of the organization are geared to implementing that architecture.

In the UK, the insurance company Thomas Miller has created a post of Director of Information to create and oversee the information architecture of the company, in parallel to existing work on information technology.

Conclusion

What is perhaps most striking about the application of information technology in financial services is the gulf between the leading-edge examples and the average. This has been described in another context as a 'chasm'. If organizations are to succeed in bridging this technology chasm, it is perfectly clear that the solutions are only marginally concerned with the technologies themselves. Technology today for most financial services businesses is a commodity. The key issue is therefore much less to do with its acquisition, than with overcoming the barriers to exploiting it fully.

The most serious competition to traditional financial institutions will come from companies without their physical assets (or it might be said) liabilities, but particularly with the information and communications expertise to develop wholly new products and delivery methods.

References

Best, D. (ed.) (1996) *The Fourth Resource* ASLIB/Gower, London.

Cheng Ann Khoo, H. (1989) 'Executive information systems: the assimilation of information technology in the banking executives' offices', MBA Dissertation, City University Business School, London.

Davenport, T. (1993) *Process innovation: reengineering work through information technology,* Harvard Business School Press, Boston.

Dockery, E. (1990) 'The strategic use of information systems technology in banking firms and building society organisations', City University Business School Working Paper, London.

Earl, M. (1994) 'Skandia International' in *Strategic Information Systems – A European Perspective* by Ciborra, Claudio and Jelassi, Tawfik (eds) (1994) John Wiley, Chichester.

Keen, P. (1991) *Shaping the Future: Business Design Through Information Technology* Harvard Business School Press, Boston.

Maglitta, J. (1995) 'Reengineering Team of the Year', *Computerworld*, Feb. 27.

McFarlan, F. W., McKenney, J. L. and Pyburn, P. (1982) 'The Information Archipelago – Plotting the Course', *Harvard Business Review* 61, January–February, pp. 145–56.

Nagel, R. and Dove, R. (1991) *21st century Manufacturing Enterprise Strategy* Iacocca Institute of Lehigh University, Lehigh, PA.

Roche, E. M. (1992) *Managing Information Technology in Multinational Corporations* Macmillan, New York.

Scott Morton, M. (1991) *The Corporation of the 1990s: information technology and organisational transformation* Oxford University Press, Oxford.

Tapscott, D. and Caston, A. (1993) *Paradigm Shift*, McGraw-Hill, New York.

Venkatraman, N. (1991) 'IT-Induced Business Reconfiguration' in Scott Morton (1991), pp. 122–58.

Winger, R. and Edelman, D. (1990) 'The Art of Selling to a Segment of One', *Business Month*, January, p. 70.

Zuboff, S. (1988) *In the Age of the Smart Machine: the future of work and power* Basic Books, New York.

CHAPTER TEN

Managing outsourcing and subcontracting[1]

Edmond Cunningham, Principal Consultant with PA Consulting Group Formerly Chairman of the Computing Services & Software Association Outsourcing Group

The outsourcing debate – determining what is core and what is not

Outsourcing is the long-term relationship (greater than one year) between a client and supplier in which the client delegates all, or a major portion, of an operation or function to the supplier.

(Input[2] Corporation, 1996)

The definition of what 'core' means to a firm varies. Some firms are of the opinion that the majority of their activities are core because they have been doing them for a long time. For the purposes of this paper I am going to view 'core' as being based on the organization's core competencies. Core competencies define a firm's long-term capabilities for adding value. A firm may have core activities which are not part of its core competencies. Hence these activities are part of the non-core competencies which firms often seek to outsource to third parties which they believe can provide a better service and return on investment.[3]

A company's strategic direction should aid a firm in determining what its core and non-core competencies are for its success in the future. The firm has to consider where it wants to be to service the future market-place. If we look at the basis of competitiveness as being set in competencies, then Hamel and Prahalad's (1994) definition of core competencies can be utilized to determine non-core. The three criteria for non-core competencies are:

1. *Non-core competencies have a low customer value* – they provide low or no contribution to the value that the customer perceives they are receiving from the firm's goods or services.

2. *They are not unique in the market-place* – meaning they are no better than anybody else's.

3. *They are not extendible into future markets* – they will not provide competitive advantage in the future market scenario.

Non-core competencies must meet one or more of these criteria to be classified in this way.

Typically firms go through an iterative strategic decision-making process (Figure 10.1), one outcome of which can be the identification of core and non-core competencies.

The core competencies are those which deliver competitiveness. Whilst the non-core competencies of a business are valuable, to turn them into core competencies will require a lot of time and energy, something that most companies do not have in abundance. The oil company BP[4] have concentrated on their core and they have outsourced and divested themselves of non-core competencies such

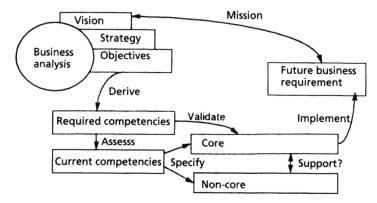

Fig. 10.1 Defining core and non-core competencies – an iterative process based on intent.

as transportation (road and sea), and business operations processes such as accountancy. So what can be done with the non-core element? The firm has to consider where it wants to be in se...

There are four options for addressing that which is considered as 'non-core' – each of which is explained below:

1. Build on what the firm has within the non-core areas to make them core competencies for future exploitation.

2. Accept and live with the lack of capability in certain non-core areas.

3. Divest the firm of non-core businesses by selling them to some-one or by shutting them down.

4. Outsource the non-core activities to a service provider whom the firm believes has the necessary capabilities to provide the activities in a more efficient and effective manner.

Option 1

If the objective of a firm is to concentrate on developing its core competencies and these were not among them, why invest in them? Why build and commit resources away from the future direction of the firm? If a firm does follow this path, then it should revise its strategy. The objective of defining the core is to concentrate on it and to make the firm more competitive in the market-place. Choosing option 1 is effectively reversing this. An industry which chose this option was the railway industry in the late nineteenth and early twentieth centuries. The railways were in the transportation business and they were decimated by road transportation. They invested in non-core areas like hotels and property. The core competency approach demands that you focus on what you do best, so that you can compete for the future.

Option 2

Accepting the status quo possibly compromises the firm's future. Effectively the firm is allowing itself to be trapped by its history. Firms have to assess constantly whether their non-core competencies are delivering value appropriate to the future market. Mainframe computer manufacturers in the late 1980s accepted the status quo for a long period before they realized that the market had changed; as a result their profitability collapsed and their viability was threatened.

Option 3

There are two types of activities which can be divested:

1. those whose output is used by the core business;

2. those whose output is not used by the core business.

In type 1. the output is a commodity in the market, it is freely available and the firm cannot or will not add sufficient value when compared to what is available in the market. For example, the car companies used to own steel mills, but they found that it was better to sell them or shut them down and buy the steel on the market, rather than to sustain their non-competitive cost structures.

In type 2. as this is not the firm's core business it is best to divest it and either get a better return through investing in the core competencies or release the value back to the shareholders. Racal did this when it released the value from Vodaphone.

Option 4

The firm should use outsourcing where the output from the current non-core activities is still required by the core business and the output is not available as a commodity in the market. The firm is effectively getting into a relationship with a service supplier who can deliver the output more effectively.

Outsourcing is an effective method of enabling firms to keep the relationship which they have with their non-core activities, while making them more efficient and increasing their value through the service provider's competencies and structural advantages.

The advantages can be in the form of:

● Greater potential when the activities are transferred to the service provider who regards them as being their core business and have the ability to develop and exploit them.

● Cost containment through forecastable prices which result from contracts that make the expenditure revenue-based through payment for a defined service.

● Service-level agreements, which can include guarantees to give the firm clear control measures and standards against which it can judge suppliers' processes, quality and performance. The firm now has contractual controls over the service provider which are often difficult to agree and harder still to enforce with in-house operations.

- More time – the firm can focus its energies on exploiting its core competencies and not have to divert time and attention to non-core activities.

- Lower costs or possibly cash can be obtained from any assets which are transferred. A service provider may purchase the firm's assets to provide the service and exploit the assets more effectively.

- Utilizing the competency of your new service providers to support the firm's core business in areas which might be outside the current remit of the relationship. This can be done to add value in areas where the firm and service supplier together have the ability to meet the market requirements but on their own they would not find it worthwhile.

Box 10.1 on the Co-operative Bank is an example of how these advantages can be gained.

Box 10.1 The Co-operative Bank

The challenge
As part of a concerted move to focus on its core value-generating activities, the management of the Co-operative Bank identified that its position in the cheque-clearing market needed strengthening through the application of additional technical and service competencies.

The process
The Bank's management, through a competitive selection process, discussed the issues with various service suppliers. They evaluated a set of discussion documents and tenders based on their own selection criteria. As part of this they held a number of senior management presentations and discussions with the suppliers about their tenders.

The solution
The Co-operative Bank chose to outsource its cheque-clearing operations to Unisys. Under the agreement Unisys would be a partner for the continued provision of the cheque-clearing service to the Bank and its clients. Unisys would provide the necessary competencies to grow the service and to introduce new technologies for services. Under the agreement, 240 Co-operative Bank staff transferred to Unisys Payment Services Ltd, which will process over 250 million cheques per year.

The benefits
The Co-operative Bank gained a partner and enabled the bank to concentrate on its core business. The Bank also reduced the cost of the service as measured against clear performance metrics. Service-level agreements were put in place which allowed the Bank to have control over the standards for process, quality and performance. The two companies now have a joint interest in extending the relationship to pursue new market opportunities using the distinctive competencies which each party possesses.

Making the outsourcing decision – hard and soft factors

Outsourcing is a relationship with a third party. The firm's management need to maintain control of the service so that they can meet their business objectives. Hence during the selection process management need to understand how they will control the service provider.

The outsourcing decision has to take into account the hard and soft factors associated with the enterprise, its environment and future positioning. These factors are described in Table 10.1.

The outsourcing process is about giving the client control of the defined service. The decision process requires that the service pro-

Table 10.1 The outsourcing decision: factors to consider

Hard Factors	Soft Factors
Scope of non-core activities to be outsourced How well can the boundary be determined? Within the boundary, can we determine the best value available?	*Cultural issues* Is 'cultural compatibility' needed between the firm and the service provider? How do we evaluate the service provider's culture?
The assets Are the assets to be transferred at book value or market value? Do we have any future requirement for these assets?	*People & stakeholder relationships* What needs to be considered to maintain these relationships? What will be the effect on the local community?
The cost structures What are they? What areas are affected?	*Expectation management* What outcome do we want and is it measurable? Can we influence the expectations of stakeholders?
Contract Are the necessary skills in-house to develop, monitor and support such a contract? Which consultancies/law firms handle this type of requirement?	*Competitive position* How will our competitors react and when? Can we exploit effectively any competitive advantages that arise from outsourcing?
The balance sheet and P&L effects What comes off the balance sheet, & what are its effect on the P&L? Will the effect on shareholder value be positive or negative in the long-term?	*Direction setting* What signals are sent out to the market by doing this? Does this limit our options for future development?

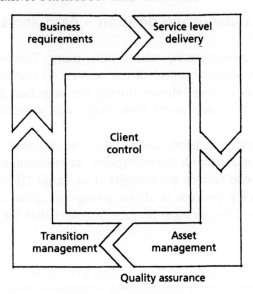

Fig. 10.2 Client control of the outsourcing.

vider has an effective management framework (Figure 10.2) which gives this control to the firm. To do this the service provider must build a clear understanding the firm's business requirements and the relationship between business performance targets and service-level delivery standards. The outsourcing process must also provide efficient and effective mechanisms to handle the transition and ongoing management of people, processes and assets. Finally the framework must be underpinned by excellent quality assurance processes.

The analysis and decision-making is best done by senior managers or board members within the organization, because of the strategic nature of the decision and the need to consider the company-wide effects.

The scope of the activity has to be 'ring-fenced' to determine exactly what will be outsourced, and to assess whether and where value is being delivered. There are two methods to use for this analysis:

● *value chain analysis* of the firm and the industry; and

● *benchmarking* against the average and best in field and other possible service providers. Benchmarking is useful to make sure that the best value is being derived from the service provider.

The assets that are involved in the delivery of non-core activities have to be assessed on the basis of their future returns. It may be necessary to transfer these assets to the service provider at a value which does not reflect their value in the balance sheet. The value is calculated only in the context of its future use by the service provider, and that might indicate an equal or higher value than is shown in the balance sheet.

The senior management of the firm has to look at the costs[5] of internal provision of the non-core activities. The correct cost structure has to be calculated for them. This can be done through the normal budgeting process. The management must also take into account the overhead costs of central services like HR, purchasing, legal and management. They should consider other views of the costs, besides the current accounting system, by looking at the costs in terms of the process and the performance their people are achieving.

The contract needs to be considered from two points of view:

1. whether the firm has the ability to negotiate, monitor and enforce it properly; and

2. what should be in it.

It is the basis for the long-term relationship with the service provider and needs care and attention so that it does not hold up the agreement timetable. If expertise is needed then the firm should hire the necessary experts (consultants and solicitors) experienced in the area.

There will naturally be an effect on the balance sheet and the profit and loss account. These are influenced by:

- how the service provision is structured;
- whether assets are transferred and at what value; and
- whether the service provider is going to purchase all the necessary assets in the future for the provision of the service.

Assuming that one of the objectives is for the profit and loss account to show higher profits in the long term, the firm must be clear on how much of this extra value is to be generated by the service provider. Identifying when and where this value will start to be generated should be part of the justification for the decision.

Part of the decision process should be to assess whether the service provider needs to be 'culturally compatible' with the firm, and if so in what areas. The best way is to ensure that the two parties are culturally compatible at the contact levels so that the translation of information between the company and service provider is made correctly. This might involve arranging joint activities between the firm and the service provider at management and operational levels. The transfer of staff to the service provider will also help to ensure the cultural compatibility by infusing into the service provider an understanding of the firm's current culture. This needs to be watched as the culture which is transferred with the employees is usually one that management is trying to alter – so the firm's management must keep the service provider in the 'change management loop' (Figure 10.3).

One of the prime areas to consider before making the decision to outsource is how to manage the people who are part of the non-core activities being transferred – this is addressed below. The relationship which the firm had with its stakeholders must also be included in the process of making the decision. The firm's existing suppliers will be affected through outsourcing, as the new service-provider will be responsible for the provision of the service. The community, too, has to be thought of, if only to make sure that the impact of outsourcing does not have an effect on the overall image of the firm. The shareholders are intrinsically being considered, because the outsourcing decision should be made to increase the value of the firm.

The firm should manage the expectations of the people inside and outside the organization about the benefits associated with outsourcing. These benefits must be clearly articulated and measured to show that value is being attained. The measurement systems should also be considered, as the internal systems may be inappropriate to the task. The in-house relationship probably never required such stringent and rigorous measurements linked to business performance of the firm as a whole.

The effect of outsourcing on the firm's competitive position has to

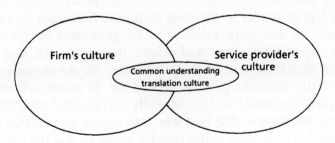

Fig. 10.3 Developing cultural compatibility.

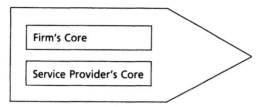

Fig. 10.4 Synergy – new opportunities to add value.

be brought into the equation. How will the firm's competitors react, and when? What window of opportunity has the firm created by outsourcing and how can it be exploited effectively? The outsourcing of component design and production by car manufacturers is a case in point. As a reaction to the close relationships which Japanese companies have with their suppliers, American and European firms started to emulate this by outsourcing to specialist providers.

The firm needs to consider the other opportunities that may appear once you introduce outsourcing, and how the market will perceive it. Outsourcing is not a leader of change – it is an enabler and it can provide for future changes through the utilization of the service provider's capabilities linked with those of the firm (Figure 10.4). When assessing outsourcing, a holistic and strategic view should be taken in order to derive the best advantage from it. The firm must consider the synergy of working with a service provider who has competencies which when combined with the firm's capabilities can enable growth for both parties. Two examples of this are Co-operative Bank and Unisys in cheque-processing, and New Holland and Andersen Consulting in logistics.

When should you redesign the processes affected by outsourcing – before or after the decision?

A firm need to have a distinct vision of where it wants to be, often described as its 'strategic intent'. Held within that vision is how each process is designed and in what form they contribute to the core competencies. Subordinate to the core are the non-core activities that support them. These may be provided by outsourcing to service providers, or they may be purchased as a commodity from a third party (Box 10.2).

This vision will help in deciding whether to redesign[6] the firm's processes before or after outsourcing. There are advantages and disadvantages associated with each choice (Figure 10.5).

As the management make this choice they may forfeit some benefits which would be available from the other option.

Increasingly, firms are adopting frameworks (Talwar, 1996) for process review and re-engineering which provide them with multiple opportunities to consider outsourcing (Figure 10.6).

● During the identification and high-level review of processes they may identify complete processes or activities which are not meeting internal performance targets and could benefit from outsourcing.

● During the evaluation against strategic direction, the firm may decide that current poor performing processes, systems and activities should be outsourced to an external supplier. Similarly the decision may be taken to shift strategic focus and outsource both core and non-core activities in order to allow management to focus time and energy on the activities considered core to the new strategic direction. In both cases the firm may ask selected service providers to work with them on the transformation process.

● At the stage of detailed analysis of current processes it may be revealed that certain processes and activities could really benefit from the extra capabilities that an external service provider could offer.

Redesign before Outsourcing
- *Advantages:*
  See the whole of the current process
  Analyse the next stages
  Adapt the processes to be outsourced specifically for the redesigned core processes
- *Disadvantages:*
  Not concentrating on core
  Not an expert in non-core arena hence not applying best practice

Redesign after Outsourcing
- *Advantages:*
  Only have core process to redesign
  Ability to concentrate and become leader
  Only new areas need to be considered, service provider provides the old processes during the transformational process
- *Disadvantages:*
  Outsourced processes may not support new redesigned process
  Linkage with old processes may prevent taking full advantage of market

---

Fig. 10.5 The choices.

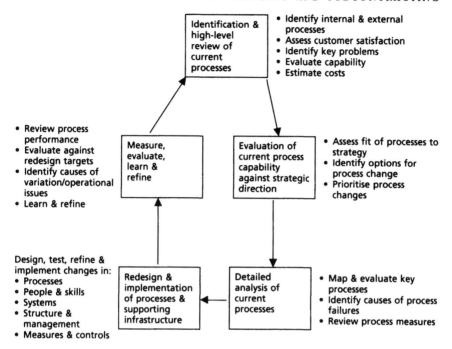

Fig. 10.6 A framework for process review and re-engineering.

● During the redesign stage, the firm may decide that the capabilities required to run the redesigned process can best be provided by an external supplier.

● Finally, once the redesigned infrastructure is in place, the measurement and learning process might highlight that additional capabilities are required to run the redesigned processes and activities to desired levels of performance and quality.

The more the service provider is involved in the transformation and the more it could influence the success of the firm in the future, the more possible it is for some part of the payment to the service provider to be linked to the firm's future success. This indicates that the service provider should have a good knowledge of the firm's market and have the necessary competencies to be a participant with the firm. This would have many advantages for the firm as it would then have a service supplier who would be very much aligned to the success of their business.

Doing the process redesign with the service provider can be a great enabler to the change management process. It will ensure that the value of outsourcing is clearly visible to the stakeholders of the firm.

Box 10.2 Dunlop Aviation

The challenge
As part of a company-wide business process re-engineering (BPR) exercise, Dunlop Aviation identified the need to focus on open platforms for its IT systems to support its future business needs. The exercise determined that if Dunlop Aviation outsourced its legacy systems operation and support services, its management information systems (MIS) staff would be able to concentrate on the migration to open systems and reduce the current IT costs.

The solution
Dunlop Aviation chose Unisys to operate its core manufacturing and financial systems until they have transferred to open systems – because of the quality and range of the services they offered, the flexibility of the proposal, and the significant cost savings in supplying IT service.

The benefits
The major benefit was to enable Dunlop Aviation MIS staff to concentrate on transferring and implementing new systems to a UNIX environment. There were also cost reductions in the provision of services and the system-response times improved by 40 per cent. Tony Scanlon, the then managing director of Dunlop Aviation said: 'The changeover went smoothly and was a seamless transition with no disruption to the operation of the business.'

Preparing people, processes and systems for outsourcing

Once the decision to outsource is taken, the next stage is the preparation of the people, processes and systems for outsourcing. There are cultural issues to be addressed; does the firm have a flexible or inflexible culture and is it receptive to the rate of change being proposed? The executive has to decide when and how this preparation needs to take place. Planning is vital for the correct and smooth preparation of outsourcing. This is planning for the transition and for the ongoing service requirement. Management of the expectations of those affected within the firm has to be considered so that the best value can be generated from outsourcing.

People

This is an issue for the whole company, not for the non-core area. The firm should expect resistance to change, it is quite normal and has to be handled correctly. For the people who are being transferred, a checklist of issues[7] should be examined under the following headings:

Capability – individual competencies, skills and capabilities.

- *Organization* – structure, management process and roles.

- *Culture* – values, behaviours and features of employing organizations.

- *Employment conditions* – terms and conditions of employment, benefits, pensions, remuneration, contracts and HR practices.

- *Representation* – trade union or staff association employee representation.

- *Career development* – career progression, training and development, job rotation.

- *Communications* – keeping employees informed of the status and intentions of the organization in respect of outsourcing and involving employees in the outsourcing process.

Staff resistance may appear as a morale issue, brought about through fear, uncertainty and doubt over what is taking place. Outsourcing should be presented as a new opportunity for the staff. They have skills which the service provider may need, such as their unique knowledge of the firm's business. Rumours will abound – these have to be acknowledged and proactively addressed. There will be union issues to handle, from both a people perspective and a political aspect. If there are people transferring to the service supplier then the legal issues associated with the transfer have to be taken care of. In the UK, the Transfer of Undertakings (Protection of Employment) regulations, TUPE[8] usually applies in outsourcing. Some of the requirements are that transferring staff should have a thirty-day consultative period prior to transfer, and that they must receive equivalent remuneration and benefits from their new employer, the service provider. It is best to assume that TUPE applies, as it makes for a better handling of employee relations, provided its function is properly presented to the staff.

A firm should handle these issues once the decision has been made, by being open with the staff and by coaching them. It is also best to carry out communications to the staff directly affected, in conjunction with the selected service provider where ever possible.

Processes

The firm's management should prepare the processes by clearly defining and 'scoping' them, as this will enable the service provider to assess properly how it can deliver the service that best meets the firm's needs and makes an acceptable return. The core processes affected will also have to be prepared for the change. They will have new relationships which have to be mapped and the formal mechanism for communications will have to be documented and communicated to the staff. Where previously they contacted an in-house organization, the whole function may have gone to a service provider. They will have to discuss any changes with a third party service provider instead of their colleagues.

Systems

The systems[9] that need preparation are the assets that may be transferred, and also the relationships with suppliers that may be moved to the new service supplier. To transfer current contracts with suppliers, the contracts have to be assigned from the firm to the service provider with the agreement of the supplier. It is usually helpful to get the agreement of the supplier, whether or not there is a legal requirement to do so. If there are capital assets being transferred, then all the issues of the sale of assets and the transfer of title to the service provider have to be addressed.

Making the transition

Once the contract has been agreed the transition takes place and the service moves from being provided in-house, to being provided by the service provider. Planning for this period should be done by the firm's staff on their own, and in conjunction with the service provider.

The service provider's plan will typically cover the following areas:

- Service delivery planning.
- Statement of work.
- Service-level specifications.
- Service-level reporting.
- Change control procedures.
- Operational procedures.

- Escalation procedures.
- Quality controls.
- Personnel planning.
- Employee communication plan.
- Benefits harmonization.
- Terms and conditions.
- Relocation.
- Staffing.
- Infrastructure planning.
- Equipment transfer.
- Security arrangements.
- Telecommunications.
- Third-party supplier contracts.
- Client liaison schedule.

The transition is very important as it sets the level of expectations for the contract. A transition plan should provide the timetable for the transfer of personnel and assets; it should address third party transfers (software licences, hardware leases, etc.) and list all assets and personnel being transferred.

During this period the firm should have a communication plan in place to keep all the employees fully informed throughout. It has to be both formal and informal: formal meetings, formal notification and reviews, and informally talking to people in the corridor. Being open and honest about the firm's intentions helps people to handle the transition period effectively and it limits the firm's costs associated with the transition by moderating any low morale and reducing the need for fire-fighting. It is important for the management to work with the staff who are the opinion-leaders to influence the perceptions of other staff, to make sure that they support the move.

Union officials can be helpful in smoothing the transition, provided they understand the implications. The management, when outsourcing, is not shutting down the business; it is outsourcing to make the company more effective and competitive.

During the transition period it is necessary for the firm's management to have regular meetings with the service supplier. A close working relationship needs to be formed during the transition process where the service provider's managers will work with the firm's managers.

The communication process for the users has to be planned and implemented prior to the transition, to answer questions and resolve important issues in a timely and effective manner. This has to be communicated to the users by the firm's managers so that on day one of the transition there is no confusion about whom to contact.

Managing the contract

The contract is the starting point of the relationship between the firm and the service provider. A well-defined contract with schedules giving the necessary information to maintain the service, will probably cover the following areas:

- The legal contract, containing obligations and warranties, dispute resolution, confidentiality, renegotiation and termination.
- Schedules, containing a statement of the work to be done, service level agreements, service management and reporting, people and assets transfers, change control process, and charges.

There are ongoing costs associated with outsourcing. The firm now has a new relationship, part of which is expressed in the formal contract and part of which is built on common understandings. The common understanding is the 'cultural fit' between the two organizations. They should have the same strategic drive so that the service provider's organization will want to service the firm, so that the firm can serve its clients. The service definition will provide that common understanding of what is required. The service level agreements will then set into place the performance, the control and the measurement mechanisms required. If the service provider does not meet the necessary performance levels the firm should have the power to penalize them for not doing so. The firm may also wish the service provider to exceed their service levels, and this may be linked to continuous improvement.

Throughout the life of the contract, changes will be necessary to meet the firm's changing business requirements. It is important that the change control mechanism should recognize this and should have built into it the necessary flexibility to enable these changes.

In order to manage the contract properly the relationship has to be managed, and the contract manager needs certain competencies to handle the relationship. The success of the relationship may depend on this individual and his or her staff having the necessary skills. The onus is on the management of the firm to select and train the contract team. They cannot abdicate responsibility for the service, although they can transfer some of the risks associated with the service delivery.

Individuals may need new competencies which they may not have at the moment. Up to this point the firm would have been involved with suppliers on a one-off transaction basis; now through outsourcing it is engaged in an ongoing long-term relationship which contractually binds the firm to its service provider. The firm's contract manager who handles the relationship with the service provider has also got to handle the relationship with the rest of the firm. In order to do this the contract manager's team has got to have the technical and behavioural competencies necessary to do both roles. A list of some of the competencies which a contract manager may require is as follows:

Technical competencies

- Business planning skills and knowledge.
- Negotiation.
- Financial management.
- Project planning and management.

Behavioural competencies

- Adaptability.
- Commitment.
- Flexibility.
- Innovation.
- Organizational integration and leadership.
- Communication and presentation skills.
- Influence and team-building.

Contract managers must have business planning skills, and be knowledgeable about the firm's business. They have to negotiate with the service provider and have financial management capabilities, as well as experience in project management and project planning. They have to be adaptable because although the aim is to get both companies culturally compatible, there will be differences. They have to be committed to the relationship, they have to be flexible and innovative, they will need to have leadership and communication skills and they must be influencers and team builders across the firms, so that they can develop a strong relationship between the firm and service provider.

The management of the contract is critical to the success of the relationship and it is important that the relationship should have the visibility in the firm to enable it to succeed. In the Box 10.3 it is clear that the firm's management believes that outsourcing is based on a close relationship.

Box 10.3 Hill Samuel Life Assurance Limited

In July 1995, Target Life Assurance Company Limited merged with Hill Samuel Life Assurance Limited, another life and pensions company in the TSB Group.

The challenge
Target Life identified four factors that were crucial to its decision:
- a low, fixed cost that could be measured against the projected revenue for the following five years;
- assured levels of service to Target Life's clients;
- experienced staff who would ensure the service levels were met; and
- minimized business risk.

The process
The firm requested competitive tenders from a number of suppliers, and through a structured process identified the best suppliers. The selected suppliers were then asked for their best and final offer.

The solution
Unisys was awarded the outsourcing contract because of its very competitive tender, and its flexible approach. Unisys initially managed the operations at Target's Aylesbury headquarters, but later in 1994, relocated staff and hardware to offices in Milton Keynes.

The benefits
During the five years of the contract, Target expects to benefit from reduced overhead costs by being able to plan for a fixed-cost IT infrastructure. Unisys has also provided guaranteed service levels, which would have been very expensive for a smaller, internal IT department. 'Outsourcing is not an abdication of the responsibility for IT by the client; it is the formation of a partnership between the client and the outsourcing supplier,' said Irene Graham, the then Managing Director of Target Life, now Deputy Chief Executive Officer of Hill Samuel Life Assurance Limited.

Handling disputes

There may come a time within the relationship when disputes arise between the firm and service provider. Resolution mechanisms for disputes should be outlined in the contract and they should provide a staged process of escalation should the dispute not be resolved. These resolution mechanisms should not prevent the firm or the service supplier from having recourse to the law when all the mechanisms have been exhausted. There should also be cooling-off periods in the resolution mechanisms, so that both sides can have time to reflect on their positions.

Mediation systems in the UK are available through independent bodies such the Centre for Dispute Resolution or the National Computing Centre. If the dispute is financial an auditor could be appointed. The root cause of the dispute should be investigated so that both sides may find a resolution. There could be an issue about the way the contract was written, it may be that neither side foresaw this particular issue arising, and some compromise could be arranged.

Disputes should be kept within the parties involved, otherwise the firm's ability to manage the situation will be reduced.

Managing consultants

The main relationship is always between the firm and its service provider. Consultants are advisers and experts in their fields who can provide best practice information on the process, and reduce risks by helping to create the best possible outcome for the firm. They have to be managed because they may get too involved in the detail and miss the overall objective of a workable relationship that brings value to both sides.

Management when outsourcing can make the decision on a strategic or on a tactical basis. From a tactical point of view the consultant can offer cost-benefit analysis on a discreet service, a selection process for the service provider, and process guidance on the construction and negotiation of the service and the contract. When there is a strategic decision being made which is linked to the strategic intent of the firm, then the consultant can advise on that linkage through understanding that intent and analysing the benefits associated not on the simple cost-benefits of the non-core activity but from the perspective of the whole firm. The consultant should help to determine the future position of the firm and consider whether outsourcing will help to achieve that position: the 'core versus non-core' debate. The firm may have different consultants for each stage of the process. It is management's responsibility to sort out any possible misunderstandings and improve the service provider.

The management of the firm should always remember that the key relationship is between the firm and the service provider; consultants may provide valuable advice but the firm's management owns the relationship, and should make their decisions based upon that.

Conclusion

Outsourcing is a valuable method of operation which can help a financial service business to respond competitively to changing customer needs. A firm's management needs to look strategically at where they want to be in the future to service their customers. The whole strategic intent of the firm has to be considered, together with how outsourcing contributes to the intent.

Outsourcing revolves around the strategic debate of what is 'core' and 'non-core' to a firm, the assumption being that the 'core' is where the firm can best compete in the future. Outsourcing of non-core activities can support the core by harnessing the competencies and economic advantages of the service provider for whom the firm's non-core is part of its core. There is an outsourcing decision process which a firm should consider. Overall the outsourcing relationship should enable the service provider and the firm to combine their core competencies to deliver competitive advantage to the client.

Notes

[1] Throughout this document, subcontracting is treated as outsourcing.

[2] The opinions expressed here are personal and do not necessarily reflect those of the CSSA Outsourcing Group, Unisys Ltd or PA Consulting Group.

[3] For a further discussion on this, see Alexander and Young (1996).

[4] From presentation given by John Cross, BP Exploration, 'Information – Business Overhead or Business Asset', Unisys Outsourcing Conference, St Paul de Vence, France (12–14 May 1993).

[5] For further information: Computing Services & Software Association (1995) Briefing Note, *IT – In-house or Outsource – the real costs.*

[6] For further information see Coulson-Thomas *et al.* (1994).

[7] Reference: Computing Services & Software Association Briefing Note (1995) *Human Resource Issues in IT Outsourcing.*

[8] For further Information: Croner (1996) *Croner's Reference Book for Employers*, pp. D109–D110.

[9] For further information: Computing Services & Software Association Briefing Note (1995) *An Introduction to IT Outsourcing.*

References

Alexander, M. and Young, D. (1996) 'Strategic Outsourcing', *Long Range Planning* Vol. 29 No. 1 pp. 116–119.

Hamel, G. and Prahalad, C. K. (1994) *Competing for the Future*, Harvard Business School Press.

Coulson-Thomas, C. *et al.* (1994) *Business Process Re-engineering Myth & Reality*, Kogan Page.

Talwar, R. (1996) *Achieving Transformation*, An Institute of Management Workshop.

CHAPTER ELEVEN

Conclusion – New era, new challenges, new solutions

Rohit Talwar, Director,
FastFuture – The Centre for
Business Transformation

This chapter is a very different sort of conclusion – in fact it is deliberately not a conclusion in the traditional sense of the word. Instead, as the bulk of this book has examined how high performing organizations have addressed change in the 1990s, I wanted to use the final chapter to look forward and think about the kinds of transformational challenges financial service organizations will face in the next century.

People, processes and performance

As we look back over the case studies and ideas presented in the book, what key messages can we take away about achieving transformation and renewal? The first and most obvious perhaps is that there can be no conclusions. For high performing organizations, transformation and renewal are now almost continuous processes driven by a combination of internal need and external imperative.

So although the journeys are far from complete, what stands out about the experiences of the case study organizations? Some of the most obvious common success factors appear to be a tight linkage between business strategy and the initiatives through which it is delivered, the use of structured approaches to drive the resulting changes and a heavy investment in training and communications. However, for me perhaps the three most striking themes that underpin all the cases are the emphasis on people, processes and performance.

Real people, real change, real results

Cases such as MLC, Midland and TSB in particular brought home the importance of gaining the buy-in of staff in order to deliver fundamental change and sustainable service improvements. Every one of the case study organizations acknowledged that people lay at the heart of their processes and that the biggest challenges they faced were those of winning over the hearts and minds of those most involved in and affected by the changes.

We saw a strong emphasis on the move away from 'telling and selling' change to staff. In their place we saw a much greater emphasis on 'involving and engaging' staff in designing and implementing the changes. The move towards participative approaches is clear recognition that people own what they help create and an acknowledgement that managerially driven designs rarely deliver operationally viable solutions. The Mortgage Express and Britannia cases are tremendous examples of the results that can be achieved when latent talent is unleashed.

The process decade

For many, the 1990s will be seen as the process decade. Processes first rose to prominence through the interest in Total Quality Management (TQM) at the end of the 1980s and start of the 1990s. Then as the TQM movement began to lose momentum around 1992–93, in sailed the good ship 'process re-engineering' with Michael Hammer at the helm.

Decrying the incremental gains of TQM, automation of poor practices and 'paving of cowpaths', Hammer – and others in his wake – urged us to look for dramatic improvements in performance by radically rethinking and redesigning our processes. While some misinterpreted BPR as simply another cost cutting technique, others saw it as a critical enabler of transformation. The cases of Britannia, MLC and WPA are all good examples of how fundamental process change can be delivered. Now, as the century draws to a close, processes are again coming to prominence as we consider how to transform ourselves to do business in a highly automated, web-enabled world.

Performance measurement

The decade saw a shift from relatively narrow historically focused, financially driven yardsticks of performance towards the use of much broader frameworks that include predictive measures. Whether re-covering from crisis in the case of Mortgage Express or seeking to achieve World Class standards as with Chemical Bank and Abbey National, this use of multi-dimensional measures of performance was clearly a critical element in every case considered.

As the understanding of performance management evolved, a number of tools and frameworks such as the Balanced Business Scorecard and Business Excellence Model emerged. The value of these mechanisms was that they helped organizations consider both the drivers and results of organizational performance. As a side effect, the concepts of best practice, world class and benchmarking all became firmly established in the business lexicon.

21ˢᵗ century themes and challenges

Now as we enter the new Millennium, an obvious question is – if we continue to focus on these themes, will it be enough to ensure continued survival and growth? If not, what new success factors will we need to master? To address these questions, we need to think about how the business environment will develop and consider the possible drivers and enablers of transformation. These themes are explored on the following pages.

As we look ahead, there can be few amongst us who do not expect the environment to become still more complex and competitive. A combination of deregulation, privatizations, mega-mergers, innovation, proliferation of distribution channels, new entrants and the growing role of the Internet will increase both the potential risks and rewards. Furthermore, the pace of developments and increasing convergence between information technology, telecommunications and multimedia are bringing about a range of previously unimaginable possibilities.

Nowhere is the impact of these forces for change more visible than in financial services – the ultimate knowledge based industry in which information is the key commodity and means of exchange. The rules of the game are changing, the winning strategies will differ markedly from those of today and the skills required to compete will be very different to those in most demand even five years ago.

For organizations and individuals alike, this fast-changing environment is throwing up a number of critical questions:

- How will these 'rules of engagement' change?

- What implications will they have for the way in which we manage and change our organizations?

- How do we as individuals develop the necessary skills required to thrive and survive in such a turbulent and uncertain world?

To help address these questions, we will examine some of the key principles of how business will work in an increasingly interconnected world and highlight some of the issues and opportunities they will create for the financial services community. Finally we will look at some practical approaches to help organizations and individuals respond to these challenges and create faster more coherent change to address them.

The emergence of the new economy

There is a growing belief amongst business gurus and business leaders alike that as we enter the 21st century and the 'Internet era' we are talking about the emergence of a new set of business rules, social behaviours and approaches to competition – in short we are talking about the emergence of a 'new economy'.

A range of traditional and online magazines, books and forums such as Fast Company, Red Herring and Wired have emerged which are all seeking to define models of the new economy and the concepts which underpin it. I have taken and expanded one of these models in order to explore its possibilities. The following list of '*10 Driving Principles for the New Economy*' is adapted from *Business 2.0*[1] – a new magazine which focuses on exploring and explaining the changing world of business. Using this model as a start point, I have set out to show how each of these principles might impact the financial services community.

Principle 1 – *Matter. It matters less*. The processing of information is more powerful and cost effective than moving physical products. Increasingly companies are being valued on intangible assets such as people, ideas and the strategic aggregation of key information driven assets. For example many now believe that the underlying value for retailers such as Tesco lies in the customer databases they are building and the extent to which these can be leveraged over the Internet to perform one-to-one marketing. Indeed at the time of writing, Tesco has announced its intention to offer free Internet access to its 10 million 'Clubcard' holders.

Massive valuations are being placed on companies playing in the Internet 'information aggregation' arena. Consider for example Yahoo! – an Internet search engine provider with limited physical assets and few employees. Yahoo's valuation rose from $400 million to $5 billion in two years because analysts believe it has developed key 'information intangibles' which will provide massive future profit streams.

Some in the financial services community have been quick to spot the opportunity for packaging and trading intellectual property assets – starting with the entertainment industry. For example, rock music artists such as David Bowie and Rod Stewart have turned their intellectual property into tradable securitized assets. They have issued bonds backed by income from sales of back catalogues and future releases.

Whilst some may see the 'Bowie Bond' as no more than an interesting diversion, others believe it is an early indicator of the emergence of a major new market sector. Some forecasters are already predicting that within ten years the value of trade in these information assets will be equivalent to or greater than that in conventional physical asset backed equities.

Principle 2 – *Space*. Distance has vanished. The world is your customer – and your competitor. Advanced telecommunications technology and the Internet enable businesses to connect with customers across the globe. However, global access brings with it global competitors. It is by no means clear who has the greatest advantage in global markets. On the one hand, we have the larger players with established infrastructures, significant financial resources and global brands.

Stacked against them are the small, but fast growing firms with minimal infrastructure, a partnership mentality, good deal-making skills and an ability to act with speed and agility in the face of opportunities and threats. In many cases, these new competitors have established themselves specifically to operate via the web and hence all their processes are designed to support web-based commerce.

The larger, more established players are discovering that brands and assets are not enough to secure advantage over the web. The number of branch locations and vice presidents count for little in an environment where customers value lower costs, convenience, creativity, ease of access and entertainment. Many firms also find that the demands of web-based competition are challenging traditional management and decision making processes. Often they require fundamental redesign in order to respond effectively and at speed to developments on the Internet.

Principle 3 – *Time*. It is collapsing. Instant interactivity is critical and is breeding accelerated change. There is a tremendous premium being placed on responsiveness and the ability to learn from and adapt to changing market needs in 'real time'. To succeed in such an environment, companies must have change management as a core competence. Dell Computer has built its entire business model around rapid response – building machines directly to buyers' specifications, analyzing customer orders to predict trends and re-engineering its systems and processes every 3–6 months. The Internet makes the 24 hour, 7 day business week a reality – indeed Citibank's marketing now tells us that 'the Citi never sleeps'.

In the case of financial services, while most welcome the opportunity, many are finding it hard to transfer transaction processing activities to the web. Even in the most re-engineered and streamlined of organizations, there is still some degree of separation between marketing, initiation of the transaction (e.g. account opening, placing a trade, etc), transaction processing, funds transfer and confirmation. In most cases these tasks are still the responsibilities of different departments or at best of different people in the same department. When dealing via the web, customers expect to complete the entire cycle from marketing through to transaction confirmation in a single online interaction. The most critical changes required here are more attitudinal than infrastructural.

To address these challenges, some firms are establishing totally separate organizations to transact web-based business. Often, many of the staff in these new businesses are drawn from backgrounds other than financial services. The aim in doing this is to avoid pre-conceived notions of 'how things are done round here'.

Principle 4 – People. **They are the crown jewels ... and they know it.** Imagination is the key battleground in the new economy. Huge premiums are being placed on ideas and the technologies, products and business opportunities they spawn. The people who create these ideas are becoming prime assets and new ways of rewarding, motivating and employing them are emerging. With the collapse of the psychological contract between employer and employee, there will be a rapid rise in the number of 'free agent' business professionals selling their talents on a project by project basis.

We have grown accustomed to the idea of agents representing the best talents in entertainment and sport. We now need to prepare ourselves for similar roles emerging in the business world. Going well beyond the traditional role of headhunters and recruitment agents, these new career managers will take on the responsibility for ensuring the best possible rewards for the managerial talent they represent.

In the US, firms such as Imcor, M2 and MacTemps are pioneering the business talent management market. What attracts them is the fact that some of the highest paid executives are now earning more in salaries, stock options and bonuses than the profits of many publicly quoted companies. Investors are attracted by the best rewards and, not surprisingly, there are already moves afoot to replicate the success of the Bowie Bond and securitize both the high potential individuals and the talent agencies that represent them.

For financial services firms the implications are twofold, firstly they will have to get used to working through agents to secure the very best talent. Secondly, a whole new market of tradable securities could open up. Whilst investing in a single individual might be considered risky, it is easy to imagine portfolio or tracker funds emerging which invest in a 'basket' of high potential earners. The challenge will be to identify the best 'stables' for grooming new talent. This opens interesting possibilities for business schools who often sell themselves on the potential future earnings of their graduates.

For example, an enterprising business school might forgo fees in exchange for a fixed proportion of all future income (salary and equity) of its graduates. These income streams could then be securitized and traded. The proceeds from the initial public offering of Harvard or LBS MBA Alumni Shares would almost certainly cover the tuition costs for the first 2–3 years before the graduate incomes start to flow in. The logic is undeniable – whilst the fortunes of their companies may rise and fall, rarely do the rewards to the executives stay flat or decline.

Consider a business school producing 150 graduates per year. Assume a conservative average salary of $200,000 over the course of an MBA graduate's 25-year career. A payment of one-half of one percent of income per year would bring in an average of $150,000 per year for each new cohort of graduates. Add in even a handful of share options, take-overs and the occasional start up such as Hotmail or Yahoo! and the potential earnings for such a fund are clearly enormous.

***Principle 5 – Growth*. It is accelerated by the network.** The Internet and e-mail can speed up dramatically the adoption of a new product or service through 'viral marketing' – network-enhanced word of mouth. Once critical mass is achieved, firms can experience exponential growth – emphasizing the importance of speed and the value of first mover advantage.

For example, Hotmail – the free e-mail service – established a user base of 10 million subscribers in 2 years. It was then sold to Microsoft for a reported $400M and is now attracting more than 100,000 new registrations per day. An interesting side effect of viral marketing is that businesses can lose control of how their brand is presented. In a networked environment, your brands are at the mercy of those who want to comment on them.

Again for financial services firms, the network effect can be a mixed blessing. News of poor performance, bad service or an ugly or 'clunky' web site can travel quickly around the Internet. In contrast, when the Prudential launched its direct savings arm Egg in 1998, news travelled fast that customers could get a quicker response by going direct through the web than by post or telephone. The resulting online traffic levels and number of account openings have grown rapidly.

***Principle 6 – Value*. It rises exponentially with market share.**
For products which help establish an industry standard, the network
effect is more pronounced. As the user base grows so too does the
product value. Indeed many companies give away the base product
to establish market share and then make their return on value added
services. A classic example of this is Netscape, the Internet naviga-
tion tool. The value of Netscape has been recognized by both the
marketplace and other players in the market – most noticeably AOL,
the Internet service provider, which purchased Netscape at the end
of 1998.

In September 1998, Dixon's, the UK's largest high street consumer
electronics retailer, launched Freeserve – its free Internet access
service. In just 20 weeks it acquired over 1 million subscribers. The
return on this investment comes in several ways including advertising revenues, charges for using Freeserve's telephone support service and a share of the call revenues from Energis which provides
the underlying network access. However, by far the biggest attraction is the potential returns on additional products and services
which can be sold to its subscribers.

The value of the data Freeserve has acquired about its subscribers
is of almost immeasurable value. Potential partners are now queuing
up to promote their products and services via this highly targeted
channel. As a result, investment analysts are having to rerate the
shares. They are adding a premium to Dixon's retailing valuation to
reflect the potential value of the income stream from an online
subscriber base that will be difficult to tempt away.

The implications for financial services firms are enormous.
The cost and timescales required to develop an equivalent on-line
subscriber base will be significant as any offering will need to be
more attractive than Freeserve's free package. Furthermore,
many will not want to become Internet Service Providers. The
alternative will be to offer their services via Freeserve, another
Internet service provider or other organizations that have built up
large databases of online users. Citibank chose the route of
partnering with Virgin.net to offer free Internet access to anyone
opening a new account.

Clearly those with the biggest and most up-to-date subscriber
bases will be able to secure the best terms from would-be partners.
A further possibility is that these Internet 'portals' or 'gateways to the
consumer' will want to add their own brand to all or most of the
services provided through them. The financial significance of these
possibilities is not fully understood by any of those involved. The

relevant infancy of the Internet as a commercial tool means that reliable usage, revenue and cost forecasts vary quite dramatically. As a result, financial service providers can only really understand the true costs of acquiring and retaining web-based customers once they have gone online.

Principle 7 – Efficiency. The middleman lives. 'Infomediaries' replace intermediaries. Theoretically, a networked world 'cuts out the middleman' and enables buyers to deal directly with sellers. However, a new breed of middlemen are emerging who help consumers make sense of the information maze. Their role is to provide added value services such as intelligent customer assistance, price comparisons and transaction processing.

From a consumer's perspective these online 'best buy' tables will be essential in helping them sort through the bewildering array of choices on offer via the web. The added attraction for the consumer will be the opportunity to link straight from the infomediary sites to those of the relevant product and service providers. The opportunity to complete transactions online helps save time by eliminating the need for telephone calls, postal delays and form filling.

Whilst those in financial services are used to independent providers as a route to market and a source of comparison, online infomediaries raise the stakes considerably. The risks lie in failing to get sufficient listings and exposure from key infomediaries – although it will be in the infomediaries' interest to ensure the quality and breadth of market information they offer.

The opportunities come in many forms. Firstly, the most agile and responsive of providers will be able to work with infomediaries to create distinctive offers, products and packages targeted to specific sectors of their customer base. Furthermore those with the most flexible systems may be able to offer integration with the intermediaries' own systems – thus enabling the immediate execution of transactions.

Some firms may even see value in becoming an infomediary – offering it as an added value service for their customers and gaining the marketing advantages from associating their brand with a high visibility financial information site. Some may also see the role of infomediary as a profitable activity in its own right.

Principle 8 – Markets. Buyers are gaining dramatic new power and sellers new opportunities. Buyers can compare products and prices at the click of a mouse and infomediaries can provide access to the best deals. Hence those with unique offerings and competitive prices will thrive while those reliant on physical barriers will see their competitive position erode rapidly.

The keys to survival here will be the capacity for rapid development and delivery of new products and services, deal-making and responsiveness to special requirements. All of these demand a high level of empowerment and devolved decision making. They also demand that the underlying settlement systems are flexible, secure and robust enough to support a constantly changing portfolio of products, features, special arrangements and deals. The need for legal compliance will become even more critical particularly when the customer and provider may be in different countries, governed by different legislative regimes.

Principle 9 – Transactions. **It's a one-to-one game.** Information is easier to customize than hard goods. Greater value is being placed on the information component of both products and services. Retailers can now make customized offers to individual customers based on the purchase information gleaned from storecards. Websites are already emerging which present themselves in a totally customized manner to each customer based on their previous interactions with the site. Clearly there is immense potential for development of customized marketing and product offerings. Electronic marketing carries with it a very different cost structure. For example, e-mail offers the opportunity for virtually free distribution of direct mail and online research surveys.

As already suggested, competing in the virtual arena will require significantly different mindsets and skillbases than those which currently predominate in the marketing functions of most financial services organizations.

The challenges lie in designing suitable marketing campaigns and messages that will solicit the desired response via e-mail – a less flexible, less visual and less colourful format than paper and television based advertising. How do you make your e-mail marketing message stand out when it arrives in exactly the same format as all other e-mails? Furthermore, how do you ensure it is not filtered out without being read by a recipient who may be receiving tens or even hundreds of e-mail messages on a daily basis?

One approach has been to give people the incentive to request e-mail correspondence from you – competitions, prize draws and give-aways being the most frequent attractions. This trend towards 'permission' based marketing and away from the traditional 'interrupt' based approaches is seen by many commentators as the way forward for marketing via digital media.

Using online permission marketing, people register to receive your marketing e-mails in return for the chance to win significant prizes. Typically, recipients are recruited via a banner advertisement on another site. Over the course of the campaign, those who have registered receive one or more e-mails. These contain a small marketing message and the competition questions – usually these are related to the product or service on offer. To answer the questions the recipient must go to the relevant web site and glean some information. Points are typically awarded for number of questions answered correctly.

The US firm H&R Block used the approach to introduce its Premium Tax service to upper income customers. It found an average response rate to outgoing e-mails of 40% and of those who participated actively in the game, 54% now understood the premium tax concept. Other similar campaigns have seen up to 25% of participants making purchases during the campaign and have seen propensity to purchase rising from 24% to 49%.

Principle 10 – *Impulse*. Every product is available everywhere. The gap between desire and purchase has closed. Branches, stores and brochures are limited in the amount of display space available – the world wide web is not. Products and services can be on permanent display 24 hours a day everywhere in the world. The gap between impulse and action is also shortening – advances in electronic commerce and product distribution systems mean that if you see something you like you can hit the buy button on screen and the product will be delivered to your home – often the next day.

In financial services where there is usually no physical product involved, the customer expectation is increasingly one of instant settlement of transactions and immediate resolution of enquiries. Whatever the challenges firms face internally, customers no longer care. We are judged not against our own previous levels of performance but against the very best of all those who provide services to our existing and potential customers. The harsh reality is that, whatever the online product, transaction, or service we may be considering or struggling with, someone will already be offering or developing it for delivery via the Internet.

Financial services via the Internet – hype, fact and fiction

Clearly, it would be easy to get washed away in wave after wave of hype and scare stories about the Internet and assume that traditional routes to market will disappear. For example, consider the views of Jacob Nielsen, author of the forthcoming book *Designing Excellent Websites: Secrets of an Information Architect.* Nielsen argues that:[2]

> *Only 10 percent of the current Fortune 500 companies will survive the next 10 years. The rest will shrivel to a fraction of their former selves, because they won't make a successful transition to the customer-centric web economy.*

However, whilst some predictions may be considered extreme, business over the Internet will be a reality for financial services providers. The sheer pace of development and the associated economics of Internet commerce make it hard to ignore. For example, volumes of traffic over the net are doubling every 90 days and estimates for trade over the web for Christmas 1998 vary from $2bn to $8.2bn.

The following statistics from *Business 2.0*[3] show the rate at which online share trading is growing:

● IDC predict that the number of US online share trading accounts will grow from 6.4 million in 1998 to 24.7 million in 2002; over the same period they forecast US online brokerage revenues increasing from $1.3bn to $5.3bn, with account acquisition costs growing from $184 to $247;

● Of those already trading online in the US, Piper Jaffray's research suggests that Charles Schwab have the biggest share with 34.2% (2 million accounts) and 29.1% of the trades made in Q3 1998. The second and third largest players are Fidelity Investments with 28.7% of accounts and 10.8% of trades and E*Trade with 9.3% of accounts and 10.4% of trades;

● Research from Intermedia Advertising Sources shows a growing level of spending on Internet advertising by online brokers, in Q1 1998 Fidelity spent $1.1M, Charles Schwab $0.8M and E*Trade $0.5M;

● Datek, currently a far smaller player with only 2.2% of online accounts, spent over $1.4M on online advertising in Q1 1998. The payback in Q3 was an average of 12.3 trades per account – more than three times more than E*Trade, four times more than Schwab and ten times more than Fidelity.

To set these figures in context, at the time of writing, Schwab's online accounts own assets worth $174 bn and represent over 35% of its total base of 5.6 million accounts. These online account holders are also a very price conscious group – research from Jupiter Communications on the primary reasons for trading online revealed that 45% were driven by lower commissions, 36% by convenience and 12% by control. Only 1% were motivated to trade online by a better service offering. Indeed, a price war is already raging between America's online brokers with commissions as low as $5 per trade.

One of the biggest attractions for transacting business online is the sheer cost differential as compared with telephone or counter based services. Various surveys have suggested that online transactions are 5–25% of the cost of the equivalent by telephone and a mere fraction of the equivalent 'over the counter' transaction. A key factor here is that cost and activity are shifted to the customer.

Infrastructure costs are also dramatically different online. To overhaul an 'online storefront' might cost anywhere from $10,000 to $50,000 and usually takes 10–20 days to complete. By contrast, the costs of overhauling a high street presence typically costs upwards of $50,000 per store and would normally take a minimum of six weeks and often requires the shop to be closed for at least part of the time with a resulting loss of business.

New entrants, new rules, new strategies

As already discussed, one of the biggest challenges to existing players may come from new entrants who are designing businesses for the Internet. Industry watchers are predicting three key types of entrant into the financial services arena. Firstly, relatively small players playing in specific niches using the Internet to design and deliver services in a fast, cheap and convenient manner. One example is E*Trade – one of the US pioneers of Internet brokerage services. As this book went to press E*Trade announced its plans to create a full-service online investment bank.[4] The new venture, E*Offering, will offer investors access to initial public offerings and the opportunity to trade stocks without going through Nasdaq market makers. The web will be used for share transactions, distribution of research information and the underwriting of stock offerings.

The second group of entrants are those who already have large customer databases, a relationship with those customers and, generally, a reputation for service and value established in another sector such as retailing. Firms such as Tesco's, Sainsbury's, Virgin and Marks and Spencer have already entered the savings market and more are expected to follow. Given the volume of subscribers generated by Internet service providers such as AOL and Freeserve, many predict it is only a matter of time before they start to offer at least a limited range of savings, credit and loan products. In most cases this type of entrant will not establish their own infrastructure for product development and transaction processing. More likely, they will cherry pick from the 'best of breed' of the existing providers or partner with new organizations established specifically to provide these third party fulfilment services.

The third group forecast to start taking a greater interest are the providers of the telecommunications, software and hardware that will facilitate electronic commerce. As competition intensifies and margins come under pressure in their traditional businesses, the attraction of these new sectors will become increasingly difficult to ignore. Given the increasing reliance on technology to underpin product development, distribution and processing even in 'conventional' financial services operations, the competences in greatest demand are those of firms like AT&T, IBM and Microsoft. Within this group one might also include providers of outsourcing and subcontracting services as described by Edmond Cunningham in Chapter 10.

In each case the entrants are not bound by traditional norms and expectations of how a financial services business should operate. Those coming from retail and telecommunications bring with them a different set of values and standards of customer service along with different approaches to management, decision making and organizational change. The net effect for many in financial services is that they are having to come to terms with an even more complex, turbulent and fast changing world where size and reputation may not guarantee survival and where the rules will be challenged, broken and redefined on a constant basis.

Understanding the net generation

Finally, we need to recognize some very distinct generational differences between today's leaders and the generation which will be defining the new rules and shaping the business landscape over the next two decades. These 18–30 year olds, termed the 'net generation', are born in a different era, operate with different value sets and have very different cultural references and aspirations to those currently at the helm. Understanding this group will be a critical success factor as they will be the architects, marketeers, customers, employees, competitors, regulators, analysts and shareholders of business in the new economy.

Managing at the 'speed of change'

How then, do we respond to the combined influences of the emergence of the new economy, the effects of deregulation and privatization and the impact of new entrants, new products and new distribution channels? Some might argue that it is impossible or pointless to even try and define long-term strategies and manage change in a coherent manner in such an uncertain environment. Whether one opts for an 'emergent and adaptive' or 'planned and deterministic' approach to defining strategy, the implementation challenges are very similar.

Irrespective of whether our organizations define strategy as a well reasoned, fully thought through five year plan or as a highly reactive series of one off initiatives, the speed with which we can turn strategy into reality is still key. The complexity and uncertainty of the environment coupled with the speed with which both existing and new competitors can act combine to place a premium on an organizations' ability to move rapidly from idea to implementation.

Managing at the speed of change demands an underlying change management infrastructure that enables us to react quickly and mobilise the right resources. With a flexible and responsive infrastructure in place, we can accelerate all aspects of the change process from defining the issue through to implementation of solutions.

Creating an infrastructure for accelerated change

Summarised below are some suggestions on the key components, tools and techniques that would form the basis of an infrastructure to support the delivery of faster, more coherent change:

Clarify the 'why and what' of change and reinforce it regularly The faster we want to implement change, the more critical it is that those involved and affected understand the reasons for the change, the desired outcomes and 'what will be different if we succeed'. One strategy for getting real understanding of the need for change is to involve staff in building simple scenarios of how the business environment might develop over the next two, three, five or ten years. Such an approach can be used at any stage in the change process.

Clearly, organizations can spend many months on defining rigorous scenarios of their environment. However, where the primary goal is a 'short, sharp, strategic shock', simple and effective scenario development can be done in less than an hour. The basic process involves defining different possible 'stories from the future' of how the business environment might develop. A number of different approaches exist for doing this.

One of the most commonly used approaches involves starting by defining the main 'driving forces' that will shape the environment. The task for those involved in the exercise is to consider how these forces might play out and combine with each to create different possible scenarios. Some exercises are more directive and specifically set out to define 'optimistic', 'pessimistic' and 'most likely' scenarios of how these forces might play out over the period in question.

To help identify driving forces, some use this variation on the PEST framework:

- Political and regulatory
- Economic
- Social and demographic
- Technological and scientific
- Environmental
- Commercial

Typical driving forces might include:

- The extent of regulatory control
- The impact of the EMU
- Dominant social values
- Take up of the Internet

- The impact of environmental regulation

- Number of new market entrants

Normally, for a short exercise, one would seek to define a maximum of 12–20 forces. The primary aim here is not intellectual rigour – simply thinking about how each of the driving forces may play out in a given scenario can have a powerful 'wake up' effect for those involved. Indeed an hour's scenario building is frequently enough to generate powerful revelations and greater recognition of the need for change.

Increasingly, project teams are using these short exercises at the start of major initiatives to make key stakeholders aware of what the environment will be like at the time the project delivers – which may well be several years away.

Agree on the vital few and ensure they are integrated
'Initiative overload' is one of the most common complaints of people at every level of the organization. The difficulty is that these initiatives may end up competing for resources and the interdependencies between them can make the situation even more complex and hinder progress. The longer the gap between idea and implementation, the more likely it is that new issues and initiatives will emerge that make it even harder to deliver the desired outcomes quickly.

Hence, if speed of implementation is genuinely a goal, management has to be disciplined and focused. The key is to prioritize from the range of possible initiatives and then select the 'vital few' which will make a real contribution to achieving business goals and on which the organization will focus its energies. It is essential that the top team review progress on each of these initiatives on a weekly basis to monitor progress and ensure that they are properly integrated.

Where the projects have been well defined and initiated correctly, these regular reviews need take no more than ten minutes per project per week and can be done face to face, by conference call or online. Using this approach, project issues can be surfaced and addressed quickly. Furthermore, when new issues and opportunities arise, the management team are better positioned to make well-informed decisions about reprioritising initiatives and re-allocating resources.

Develop a personal support network The pressures of delivering major change initiatives can be immense. Many managers find it uncomfortable talking about these challenges to peers within the business, particularly if they are one of the causes of stress! Hence, many organizations now acknowledge this and encourage their managers to look outwards and join external networks and associations. The aim is to identify peers who are also undertaking significant changes or have already done so and with whom one can share issues and talk through alternative solutions.

Invest in core change skills High performing organizations acknowledge that the skills required to transform an organization are fundamentally different to those required to manage day-to-day operations. Furthermore, the lack of relevant skills is often cited as a key cause of the delay or failure of major change initiatives. Recognising these issues, Mortgage Express trained a third of their staff in problem solving, facilitation and coaching so new change initiatives could be launched quickly.

Use after action reviews Given the pace at which organizations must change themselves, they cannot afford to wait until the post-implementation review to learn about potential improvements. Nor can they afford to pursue a path of action regardless of the impact. To address this, best practice firms are adopting the concept of 'after action reviews' as used by the army and police in conflict situations. The basic principle is a simple one – review tasks as they complete, feedback the learning and make any necessary corrections to the approach immediately.

One approach is to have the change teams and line staff involved spend at least a half-hour together per week talking through the activities undertaken this week. The aim is to review progress, discuss how tasks were performed, focus on the learning and examine causes of successes and problems. The key is to review the learning whilst it is fresh in people's memories and can still influence the conduct of the change process.

Stimulate and challenge The sheer weight of internal documentation and correspondence to be processed on a weekly basis can lead to a strong inward focus. The challenge is to ensure that there is sufficient external stimulus coming in to avoid complacency. Conferences, benchmarking, networking forums and training courses can help. However, publications and the Internet usually provide the cheapest and most easily accessible 'window on the world'. For those particularly interested in the New Economy, one could try magazines like Fast Company, Harvard Business Review, Long Range Planning, The Futurist and *Business 2.0* and online newsletters such as Wake Up, Fast Take, Fortza (see Appendix for a list of references).

Build a network of devil's advocates   As hard as we may try, for those of us on the inside, it can be extremely difficult to view the organization from a different perspective and genuinely challenge the rules. To help overcome this I encourage firms to identify people in different parts of the business and from the outside world who are willing to come in and ask naive, obvious and difficult questions. This can be a key role for members of the peer network described above.

Use participative, collaborative methods   In Chapter 1 I introduced the idea of participative large group workshops as a means of accelerating the change process. The aim is to put the 'whole system in the room' with a clear objective of achieving an agreed outcome that can be delivered at speed. This buy-in to the goal is critical. A common objective forces people to focus on the business issue, the customer need and the competitive imperative rather than the internal, departmental, hierarchical and political issues that can hinder project progress.

Develop Online Project Memory/Communications   Over the course of any large project a number of issues will be addressed and a huge volume of documentation can be generated. Furthermore, considerable effort is often devoted to explaining the same information to different interest groups. The technology is now available to help address some of these issues using the web, Intranet, e-mail and other forms of group support technology. The basic principle is to use the technology to make project information widely available and easily accessible.

For example, the US telecommunications company Bell South is using a combination of these technologies to support a major transformation programme. They have provided facilities for online conferences, project noticeboards, common access to project files, an online surgery and a frequently-asked-questions (FAQ) database. Those that want to can join e-mail groups which discuss key topics and interested parties can register to receive daily or weekly digests of all information posted to the various online forums.

Create a resource base   Significant amounts of time can be consumed in identifying suitable project support resources. The knowledge gathered can then dissipate when the project ends. This can be avoided by developing a central change management library of videos, books, case studies, CBT materials, problem solving approaches, techniques and toolkits, magazines and books that can be used to support training and help in the generation of ideas.

Make fun part of the process Over the course of a large project, one of the biggest challenges is maintaining high levels of morale, energy and creativity. Whilst some of us may find it hard to acknowledge the importance of 'fun', most would agree that the presence of 'misery' rarely leads to a great outcome. The use of a variety of simple techniques can help keep the process fresh. Part of the project resource base should be a variety of toys, games, unusual items, brainstorming approaches and creativity techniques that will help trigger ideas, break restraining paradigms and liberate the imagination of those involved.

Learn storytelling Most business communication is in the form of stories. Good story telling is an art and the best leaders are motivators who are often excellent storytellers – spend a morning at a nursery to learn from the professionals.

Help people develop personal change strategies One of the most frequently cited causes of failure on large-scale transformation initiatives is a failure to identify and think through all of the relevant stakeholder considerations at the outset. The stakeholders are all those who have an interest in the change either because they are directly involved, e.g. an employee, or because there is a knock on impact, e.g. the manager of another department whose work processes will be affected.

Most of us have become quite adept at identifying and planning the physical changes, e.g. new processes, systems, department structures, working areas, jobs, roles and training requirements. However, the stakeholder considerations are usually less tangible. These are typically tied up in organizational politics, conflicting goals and agendas and concerns over potential gains and losses from any impending change.

A second issue is that whilst many of us can articulate the need for change and highlight the issues that need to be addressed, we often struggle to describe what the outcome will look like and what will be different when we finish. Hence it can be very effective to have people start a project by thinking about its outcomes and what will have changed if it is successful. Again the stakeholder approach is a powerful way of approaching the question, i.e. what will the key stakeholders be doing, thinking, saying and experiencing if the project succeeds. Even a ten-minute discussion amongst key project sponsors usually highlights some very different 'going-in positions' on goals, expectations and assumptions.

To address these challenges, the following simple technique can be used to help people literally 'step through' an entire change process before they undertake it. The basic principles of this approach are that the more we use the process and use it to 'rehearse the future' the clearer we can be about the desired outcomes and the better equipped we are for the different possibilities that might emerge during the course of the change:

1. Think of a major change that you need to implement at work or in your private life;

2. Imagine a line stretching out in front of you with the present day at the start of it and the completed change at its end point;

3. Walk to the endpoint of the line – the point in the future when that change has been implemented successfully;

4. Given that the change has been successful, think about the key stakeholders – the main parties involved in and affected by the change – what will be different for them if the change is implemented successfully, what will they be saying, thinking, doing, feeling and believing?

5. Step back into the present day;

6. Now walk forward from the present towards the change you have just envisaged, considering the critical actions you will have to take at each step along the way in order to achieve the outcomes you envisaged at step 4;

7. When you have reached your destination, turn and look back over the path you have just travelled – what are your observations about the time it took, the way it was achieved and the issues encountered en route? Did you achieve the desired outcomes? If not, why not? What were the major obstacles?

8. Looking back over the path you have just travelled, what changes would you make, either to the goals or the way in which you will implement them? Where might you need to devote more time and attention?

9. Imagine you have now been joined by a trusted and impartial coach who knows your strengths and weaknesses – what advice would be given to you about implementing the proposed change?

10. (Optional) Return to the present day and walk through the steps in the change process again trying to act on the learning from steps 8 and 9 above

11. Review the outcomes and repeat steps 6–10 if required.

The suggestions made here are by no means exhaustive – the aim is to provide the basic elements of the toolkit to which you will no doubt add as you embark on your own journeys of transformation and renewal.

Conclusions – A 21ˢᵗ century survival guide

If we revisit our earlier discussion, what could we conclude as being the key themes and challenges that will dominate the management agenda in the coming decade? Firstly, there can be no doubt that we are entering a combat zone where ideas are the heavy artillery. The ability to generate ideas, break paradigms and look for the 'white spaces' will be a major differentiator. To deliver these ideas will require a combination of flexibility, a capacity for continuous change and a supporting change architecture that enables us to bring ideas to fruition quickly.

Perhaps the most critical ability and the one which will allow both organizations and individuals to survive and thrive in turbulent times is one which is also most at odds with the way in which most of us have developed as managers and professionals. I believe the single biggest factor that will differentiate high performers from the chasing pack will be their ability to embrace and accommodate that which we've spent most of our careers trying to eliminate. Indeed, I look forward to the day when our appraisal forms place greatest emphasis on three key words – *tolerance of uncertainty*.

References

1. 10 Driving Principles of the New Economy, *Business 2.0 Magazine*, Premiere Issue, Summer 1998, Imagine Media, www.business2.com
2. Survival in the E-Economy, *Internet Business Magazine*, December 1998 p15, Ziff-Davis, www.ibizmag.com
3. Internet at a Glance, *Business 2.0 Magazine*, January 1999 p115. Imagine Media, www.business2.com
4. E•Trade Teams up to Underwrite Stocks, *The Industry Standard*, January 25ᵗʰ 1999 p27, Internet Industry Publishing, www.thestandard.com

Appendix – Resources for transformation and renewal

When organisations embark on major transformation and renewal initiatives, one of the most frequently asked questions is 'where do we look for ideas, cases, resources and inspiration?' The list below is designed to provide some initial references – many of the Websites will provide further links to other sites and publications. Please note that whilst every effort has been made to ensure the accuracy of the references provided, the website addresses can and do change quickly and so we cannot guarantee their accuracy.

1. Useful websites/addresses

Benchmarking/Quality Management

1. American Quality and Productivity Centre – http://www.apqc.org/
2. Baldridge info – www.nist.gov
3. Baldridge – http://www.finnevo.fi/ and http://www.finnevo.fi/LINKS.HTM
4. Benchmarking Centre – http://www.ozemail.com.au/~benchmrk/

5. European Foundation for Quality Management – www.efqm.org
6. International Benchmarking Centre – http://www.ibc.apqc.org
7. Quality Management List – quality@pucc.bitnet
8. TQM – www.dbainc.com and brint.com.

Business Transformation/Change Management/BPR

9. BPR Online Learning Centre – http://www.prosci.com/ index.htm
10. Brint – BPR & Innovation Site – http://www.brint.com/BPR.htm
11. Business Transformation Books – http://www.vision-nest.com/ btbc/index.shtml
12. Business Transformation Reading List – http://www.co-i-l.com/ cbw/ReadingList.html
13. Computer Information Centre BPR Site – http:// www.compinfo.co.uk/tpbpr.htm
14. Department of Defense BPR Site – http://www.dtic.mil/dodim/ bpr.html
15. DoD College of Innovation – BPR Resources – http:// www.dtic.mil/c3i/bprcd/mwelcome.htm
16. Enterprise Re-engineering – BPR Resource Centre – http:// www.reengineering.com/
17. International Society for Enterprise Engineering – http:// www.iseenet.org/
18. Measuring the Financial Cost of Organizational Conflict – http://www.mediationworks.com/mti/cost.htm
19. Mithya Institute – http://www.mithya.com/
20. MIT Tools for Inventing Organisations – Tom Malone's Handbook – http://ccs.mit.edu/CCSWP198/
21. NASA Change Management Site – http://www.hq.nasa.gov/ office/hqlibrary/hotpicks/mgt/change.htm
22. Organisational Transformation / BPR – http:// duticai.twi.tudelft.nl/lists/bpr-l/ and listserver bprl@duticai.twi.tudelft.nl
23. Proscii – BPR Guide – www.prosci.com/modl.htm
24. Proscii Online BPR Resource Centre – http://www.prosci.com/ bpr_ahl.htm
25. Texas University – BPR in the Future – http:// cism.bus.utexas.edu/issues/issue24/iindex.html
26. WARIA – Workflow and Re-engineering International Association – http://www.waria.com/

Creativity/Innovation

27. Buffalo University Site – http://www.buffalostate.edu/~cbir
28. Computerworld Smithsonian IT Innovation Awards – Case Studies – http://innovate.si.edu
29. Creative Advantage – Online Creativity Newsletter – http://www.demon.co.uk/advantage/create/index.htm
30. Creativity List – create-l@listserv.acsu.buffalo.edu
31. Creativity Web – http://www.ozemail.com.au/~caveman/Creative/index.html
32. Flash! – http://www.flash.net/
33. Fortza! – Focus on Business Newsletter – fortza-owner@sparklist.com
34. Mental Olympics – http://www.mindsports.com
35. Worldwide Brain Club – A User Manual for the Mind – http://www.silkwood.co.uk/wwbc

Facilitation

36. DoD College of Innovation Facilitation Skills Course – http://www.dtic.mil/c3i/bprcd/4122.htm
37. Facilitation Factory – http://www.facilitationfactory.com/
38. Facilitator Central – http://hsb.baylor.edu/html/fuller/fac/
39. Group Facilitation list – grp-facl@cnsibm.albany.edu
40. Group Facilitation Site – http://uacsc2.albany.edu/~GRP-FACL/
41. Institute for Co-operative Communication – http://www.escape.ca/~rbacal
42. Institute for Cultural Affairs – http://www.icaworld.org/
43. International Association of Facilitators – http://hsb.baylor.edu/html/fuller/iaf
44. Online Guide To Active Reviewing / Debriefing – http://www.users.globalnet.co.uk/~rogg/
45. Storytelling – http//www.storytelling.co.uk
46. Team Building – http://www.neo-humanista.org

Futures/The New Economy

47. Blur – supporting site for the book – http://www.blurt.com
48. Business2.0. Magazine – www.business2.com
49. City University Business School – http://web.city.ac.uk/~sf329/sitemenu.html

50. Digital People – not for profit recruitment agency for new media – interesting new media events – http://www.digitalpeople.org/
51. Earthspace – http://earthspace.net/
52. Fast Company Magazine – www.fastcompany.com
53. Fast Company Free Trial Offer – http://www.fastcompany.com/ecom/subscribe/offer.html
54. FastFuture – The Centre for Business Transformation – http://www.fastfuture.com
55. Online Dealmakers – www.fourleaf.com
56. World Future Society – http://www.wfs.org/wfs
57. Zdnet – http://www.zdnet.com/

Information Technology

58. BBC Millenium site – http://news.bbc.co.uk/hi/english/special_report/1998/03/98/millenium_bug/default.htm
59. Canada's Y2K Assessment – http://www.canadaone.com/magazine/global-070698.html
60. Christian Science Monitor Y2K Perspective – http://www.csmonitor.com/cgi-bin/avwebsearch
61. Forrester Research – www.forrester.com
62. Infonortics IS Research & Events / Virtual Communities Site – www.infonortics.com
63. Social Impact of IT – www.cs.cmu.edu/afs/cs.cmu.edu/user/kraut/www/kraut.html
64. World Bank Y2K Site – http://www.worldbank.org/infodev/y2k.html
65. Y2K Information Centre – http://www.year2000.com/

Internet/Web/Electronic Commerce

66. Brint E-Commerce – http://www.brint.com
67. E-commerce World – http://ecworld.utexas.edu/
68. Internal and External Communications Multimedia Training – http://www.iec.com
69. Premonous – http://www.premenos.com/Resources/lists/
70. Multimedia Training Course – http://zeus.slais.ucl.ac.uk/www/index.htm
71. Roger Clarke's E-Commerce Site – http://www.anu.edu.au/people/Roger.Clarke/EC/

72. Tom Ho's E-Commerce site – http://e-comm.internet.com/
73. Veo Systems E-commerce Site – http://www.veosystems.com/

Knowledge Management

74. Brint Knowledge Management – http://www.brint.com/km/whatis.htm
75. Knowledge Ecology Fair – http://www.tmn.com/kefair/index.htm
76. Knowledge Ecology University – http://www.KnowledgeEcology.com/keu/
77. Knowledge Management Consortium – knowledgeconsortium@km.org
78. Knowledge Management Net – http://www.ozemail.com.au/~caveman/Creative/index.html
79. Outsights Knowledge Base – http://www.outsights.com/

Learning Organisations/Leadership/Organisation Development

80. Action Research – www.enhanced.designs.com/actnet/
81. Appreciative Enquiry – www.appreciative-inquiry.org
82. Association of Leadership Educators – http://www.aces.uiuc.edu/~ALE/
83. Brint Learning Organisation – http://www.brint.com/OrgLrng.htm
84. Enlightened Leadership – http://www.enleadership.com/articles.html
85. Hallmark Cards Learning Organisation Site – http://www.hallmark.com/ourcompany_bin/corporate/brands/gold.asp
86. Humanistic Resources / Common Good – http://www.commongood.org/resource.html
87. Learning Organisations – http://www.learning-org.com
88. Lessons in Leadership – http://www.wyn.com/intro-intl.html
89. MIT Learning Organisation Site – http://learning.mit.edu
90. Organisational Development List – odnet@tmn.tmn.com
91. Organisation Development Network – http://www.odnet.org
92. Organisation Development Resource List – http://www.odnet.org/prodn/prodninetin.html

93. Workplace Spirituality – http://www.spiritweb.org/Spirit/ workplace-l.html

Marketing

94. Don Peppers & Martha Rogers 1 to 1 Marketing site – http:// www.1to1.com
95. Hi Tech Marketing – http://www.bayne.com/wolfBayne/ htmarcom/default.html

Online Magazines

96. HotWired – http://www.hotwired.com
97. Industry Week – http://www.iwgc.com/
98. Red Herring – http://www.redherring.com/home.html
99. Wired Online – http://www.wired.com

Strategic Management

100. Arizona University Anticipating the Future – ag.arizona.edu/ futures
101. Financial Forecast Centre – http://www.neatideas.com/ economics
102. Foresight Programme – www.foresight.gov.uk.
103. Global Business Network – http://www.gbn.org/home.html
104. Global Management Forum – http:// www.globalmanagement.com
105. UK Strategic Planning Society Tel 44 171 636 7737 Fax 44 171 323 1692 www.sps.org.uk
106. University of Maryland Scenario Planning – bsos.umd.edu/ icons/scenario.htm

Web Fundamentals

107. A tour of the Internet. The Crispin Tourbus has a series of stops for different ways of using the Internet http:// www.tourbus.com/archives.htm
108. Scholarly Societies Project (Listing of scholarly and professional associations). http://www.lib.uwaterloo.ca/society/ overview.html

109. Professional Associations – http://www.clay.net/profass.html
110. Internet Discussion Groups Listing – http://www.tile.net/tile/listserv/index.html
111. World Wide Consortium – http://www.w3.org
112. Vision Internet Services (guide for new users) – http://www.vision.net.au/new-users/new-user.htm
113. Netiquette Guidelines – http://www-dcn.fnal.gov/General/rfc1855.txt

2. Books

Blur – The Speed of Change in the Connected Economy – Stan Davis & Christopher Meyer – Capstone Books
Britain 2010 – The PSI Report – Jim Northcott – Policy Studies Institute
Hope is not a Method – Gordon R. Sullivan & Michael V. Harper – Times Business Books
The Art of the Long View – Peter Schwartz – Century Business
The Death of Competition – James F. Moore – Wiley Books
The Fifth Discipline – Peter M. Senge – Doubleday Currency

3. Magazines, journals and associations

Business2.0. Magazine – www.business2.com
Fast Company Magazine – Tel 1 303 604 1465
Harvard Business Review Tel 44 1858 435 324 Fax 44 1858 468 969
Institute for Research on Learning USA – 1 415 496 7900 / Fax 415 496 7957
Leader to Leader – Drucker Foundation/Jossey-Bass – Tel 1 415 433 1767 email subinfo@jbp.com
US Association for Quality and Participation – Publishers of Quality and Participation – Tel 1 513 381 1959 UK
Involvement & Participation Association Tel 0171 354 8040 Fax 0171 354 8041
UK Strategic Planning Society – Long Range Planning Journal – Tel 44 171 636 7737 Fax 44 171 323 1692
Wired Magazine – Tel 00 1 800 276 8506

World Future Society USA – Publishers of Futurist Magazine – Tel 1 301 656 8274/Fax 1 301 951 0394

To receive regular updates on this list please email Rohit Talwar at robit@fastfuture.com

Index

Abbey National
  activity-based costing 40–42
  Balanced Business Scorecard 33–5
  benchmarking 38–40
  Branch Best Practice Review 42–4
  company structure 30–31
  corporate history 30
  flotation 30, 32
  leadership and change 37–8
  procurement 45–7
  service quality 47–50
  Strategic Performance
      Improvement 35–7
  value-based management 33
activity-based costing 40–42
arrears collection processes 85–8
  individuals and roles 89–90
  technology 90–91

Balanced Business Scorecard 14–15,
      190
  at Abbey National 33–5
  at Mortgage Express 65
benchmarking 38–40, 68, 123–4, 172
Best, D. 163
Birmingham Midshires 28
BPR see Business Process
      Re-Engineering (BPR)
Branson, Richard 52
Britannia Building Society 85–94

arrears collection processes 85–6,
      87–8
  individuals and roles 89–90
  technology 90–91
  business process re-engineering 87,
      93–4
  company structure 86
  economic recession effects 86–7
  strategy 88
  targets 91
business excellence model 61–2, 190
Business Process Re-Engineering
      (BPR) 15–25
  approaches 23–5
  business re-engineering 19
  Chemical Banking Corporation
      124–6
  definition 15–16
  framework 24
  human resource departments 125–6
  ongoing renewal 23
  principles 16–17
  process improvement 17–18
  process re-engineering 18
  transformation of the business 19–23
  in TSB 269–70

Caston, A. 158
Centre for Dispute Resolution 185
Champy, James 15–16

Chemical Banking Corporation 95–112
  benchmarking 123–4
  business process re-
      engineering 124–6
  company structure 95–6
  controls 117–19
  derivatives processing 113–15, 121–3
  global organization 100
  internal customer charter 110
  merger with Chase Manhattan 132–3
  mind map 96–7
  mission statement 100–102
  model for managing change 102–104
  operating environment 97–8
  optimization review processes 119–
      23
  product innovation 104–106
  programme management 131–3
  project managment 126–31
  quality programme 106–12
  risk management 115–16
  securities settlement process 120–21
Cheng Ann Khoo, H. 154
Co-operative Bank
  outsourcing 170
competencies
  core competencies 166–70
complaints 54–5, 55–6
consultants 185–6
contract management 182–4
controls 117–19
core competencies 166–70
  see also competencies
culture
  perceptions of 72–3
Cunningham, Edmond xxv
customers
  complaints 54–5, 55–6
  importance of loyalty 52–3
  satisfaction policies 54–6, 79–81

Davenport, T. 154
derivatives 113–15, 121–3
distribution networks
  information technology 161–2
Dockerty, E. 158, 162
Dove, R. 159
Dunlop Aviation 178

Edelman, D. 157
electronic cash 160–61
employees
  opinion questionnaires 70–71
  satisfaction policies 57, 81–2

feedback 70
Fries, Brian xxv–xxvi

Hamel, G. 167
Hammer, M. 15–16
Heskett, J.L. 53
Hill Samuel Life Assurance Limited
      184
Holtham, Clive xxvi–xxvii
human resources
  re-engineering 125–6

IBOS (inter-bank on-line system) 162
information technology (IT)
  building new capabilities 149–52,
      158–9, 162–4
  computer-based systems 155–7
  and delivery channels 161–2
  electronic cash 160–61
  legacy systems 152–4
  management concerns 158
  potential identification 154–5
  product-based systems 155–7
innovation 104–106
internal service quality 57–8
Internet 200–203

Kaplan, R.S. 14
Keen, P. 149

leadership 37–8, 65–7, 115–16
Littlewood, Ken xxvii–xxviii
Lloyds TSB Group 22–3

McFarlan, F.W. 149
Maglitta, J. 159
Manufacturers Hanover Bank 153
market pressure 4
Marks and Spencer 52
Midland Bank 53–9
mission statements 64–5
  Chemical Banking Corporation 100–
      102
Mondex 160
Mortgage Express 61, 63–5
  Balanced Business Scorecard 65
  business results 82–3
  customer satisfaction 79–81
  employee satisfaction 81–2
  impact on society 82
  leadership 65–7
  mission and values statement 64–5
  outsourcing 73–4
  people management 70–73

Process Review and Management Project (PRAM) 74–5
resource management 73
Total Quality Management (TQM) 76–9
Murley, Tim xxviii

Nagel, R. 159
National Computing Centre 185
Norton, D.P. 14

objectives 126
optimization review processes 119–23
outsourcing 73–4, 170
  contract management 182–4
  decision factors 171–5
  determining core competencies 166–70
  disputes 185
  managing consultants 185–6
  preparation
    of people 178–9
    of processes 179–80
    of systems 180
  redesigning processes 175–8
  transition period 180–82

participative approaches to change 25–8
people management 70–73
performance
  process improvement 17–18
  see also Balanced Business Scorecard
planning
  and project management 127–8
  strategic planning 68
Prahalad, C.K. 167
Process Review and Management Project (PRAM) 74–5
processes
  improvement 17–18
  preparation for outsourcing 179–80
  re-engineering 18, 189
  redesigning 175–8
procurement 45–7
programme management 131–3
project management 126–31
  life cycle methodology 129–31

quality programmes 56–7, 106–12
  business excellence model 61–2
  internal 57–8

measuring 55–6
Total Quality Management (TQM) 18, 76–9

re-engineering see Business Process Re-Engineering (BPR)
regulation 4, 98
Reicheld, F. 53
resource management 73–4
risk management 115–16
Roche, E.M. 153
Ross, Leslie xxviii–xxix

Sasser, W. 53
Scott Morton, M. 150
securities industry
  settlement process 120–21
service chain model 53–9
  customer satisfaction 54–6
  employee satisfaction 57
  integration of activities 58–9
  service profit chain 53
  service quality 47–50, 56–7, 106–12
  internal 57–8
Skandia 155
Strategic Performance Improvement (SPI) 35–7
Strategic Technology and Research (STAR) 153
synergy 175

Talwar, Rohit xxix
Tapscott, D. 158
teams
  and project management 127
Thomas Miller 163–4
Total Quality Management (TQM) 18, 76–9
TSB 22–3

value chain analysis 172
value-based management 33
Venkatraman, N. 150
Virgin Group 52

Welch, Jack 60
Western Provident Association (WPA) 20–21
Winger, R. 157

Zuboff, Shoshana 150, 151

Printed and bound by CPI Group (UK) Ltd, Croydon, CR0 4YY

08/05/2025

01864781-0001